John Macmurray

Selected Philosophical Writings

Edited and Introduced
by Esther McIntosh

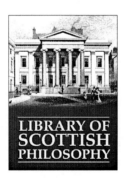

ia

IMPRINT ACADEMIC

Published in the UK by Imprint Academic
PO Box 200, Exeter EX5 5YX, UK

Published in the USA by Imprint Academic
Philosophy Documentation Center
PO Box 7147, Charlottesville, VA 22906-7147, USA

ISBN 0 907845 738

A CIP catalogue record for this book is available from the
British Library and US Library of Congress

Contents

Selections reprinted with kind permission from the
John Macmurray Trust

Series Editor's Note

The principal purpose of volumes in this series is not to provide scholars with accurate editions, but to make the writings of Scottish philosophers accessible to a new generation of modern readers. In accordance with this purpose, certain changes have been made to the original texts:

- Spelling and punctuation have been modernized.
- In some cases, the selected passages have been given new titles.
- Some original footnotes and references have not been included.
- Some extracts have been shortened from their original length.
- Quotations from Greek have been transliterated, and passages in foreign languages translated, or omitted altogether.

Care has been taken to ensure that in no instance do these amendments truncate the argument or alter the meaning intended by the original author. For readers who want to consult the original texts, full bibliographical details are provided for each extract.

The Library of Scottish Philosophy was launched at the Third International Reid Symposium on Scottish Philosophy in July 2004 with an initial six volumes. Attractively produced and competitively priced, these appeared just fifteen months after the original suggestion of such a series. This remarkable achievement owes a great deal to the work and commitment of the editors of the individual volumes, but it was only possible because of the energy and enthusiasm of the publisher, Keith Sutherland and the outstanding work of Jon M.H. Cameron, Editorial and

Administrative Assistant to the Centre for the Study of Scottish Philosophy.

Acknowledgements

Grateful acknowledgement is made to the Carnegie Trust for the Universities of Scotland for generous financial support for the Library of Scottish Philosophy in general, and to Mr George Stevenson for a subvention for this volume in particular.

Acknowledgement is also made to the University of Aberdeen Special Libraries and Collections for permission to reproduce the engraving of the Edinburgh Faculty of Advocates from *Modern Athens* (1829) and to the John Macmurray Trust for permission to reprint the extracts and the cover photograph.

Gordon Graham
Aberdeen, June 2004

Introduction

A Brief Biography

John Macmurray was born on 16 February 1891 in Maxwelltown, Kirkcudbrightshire, Scotland. Macmurray's parents were devout Calvinists and sought to raise Macmurray and his siblings according to strict religious ideals, which influenced him greatly. When Macmurray was eight years old, the family moved to Aberdeen and it was here that he first met Elizabeth (Betty) Hyde Campbell (the sister of a school friend), who later became his wife. Macmurray was educated firstly at the Aberdeen Grammar School and subsequently, having gained a scholarship, at Robert Gordon's College. In 1909 he registered for an MA degree in Classics and Geology at the University of Glasgow. At this time he fully intended to follow his father's wishes by becoming a missionary; hence, he joined the Student Volunteer Missionary Movement. He became a member of the Student Christian Movement as well, and it was here that he happened upon a more flexible form of Christianity than he had known previously. In his final year at Glasgow University, Macmurray was turned down by the China Inland Mission, on the grounds of ill-health. By this time, however, he had become increasingly disillusioned with dogmatic Christianity, having discovered that many traditional Christian doctrines cannot be found in the Bible.

In 1913 Macmurray graduated from Glasgow University with First Class Honours. He was keen to study philosophy and took up the place of Snell Exhibitioner and Newlands Scholar at Balliol College, Oxford. Here Macmurray began studying Greats under the tutelage of A.D. Lindsay, but war broke out before he had completed the course. Out of consideration for pacifist principles, Macmurray enlisted as a nursing orderly. By 1915 he was at the front with the Royal Army Medical Corps, where wounded soldiers received treatment on the basis of their ability to go back into combat. Hence, under the impression that he was already contributing to the fighting effort, Macmurray became a Lieutenant with the Queen's Own Cameron Highlanders. He was granted three days leave in the autumn of 1916 to marry Betty, but had to return to the Battle of the Somme. He was not there long before being sent back to England with a broken ankle. While he was recovering, he gave a sermon in North London, urging reconciliation rather than vengeance. In response to the hostile reception his message prompted, he made the decision to reject membership of any Christian Church.

When Macmurray returned to the frontline he was sent to the Battle of Arras, where he was severely wounded and the rest of his company were killed. He was invalided home and awarded the Military Cross for bravery. When the war was over, he returned to Balliol College, Oxford to sit his examinations in Greats and to begin his career as a professional philosopher. He remained at Balliol as John Locke Scholar of Mental Philosophy for less than a year, having acquired a Lectureship in Philosophy at the University of Manchester (1919–21). Two years later he had taken up a post as Professor of Philosophy at the University of Witwatersrand, Johannesburg (1921–2), where he used his free time to campaign for improved housing for black South Africans. Before long he was invited back to Balliol College as Fellow and Classical Tutor (1922–8). In 1923 Macmurray gave the Jowett Lectures, with the title 'The Historical Approach to Modern Idealism', and in 1924 he was elected to the membership of the Aristotelian Society. From the articles and lectures that Macmurray gave during his time at Oxford, it is apparent that he had already begun work on the issues that were to dominate his philosophical career; in particular, he began to focus on a germinal form of his concern with the concept of the person.

Macmurray left Oxford to take up the post of Grote Professor of Mind and Logic at University College, London (1928–44), where his inaugural address was entitled 'The Unity of Modern Problems'. Once in post Macmurray quickly reorganized the department: he decided to encourage the students to participate in seminar discussion; he established intercollegiate teaching of philosophy with the other London colleges; and he was instrumental in recruiting A.R.C. Duncan as a colleague. In addition, the Academic Assistance Council asked Macmurray to referee the work of refugee scholars fleeing Germany; hence, he was introduced to Theodor Adorno, and subsequently engaged with Karl Popper, Gabriel Marcel and Martin Buber. Moreover, Macmurray was receiving invitations from North American and Canadian universities, which led to a three month tour in 1936 that included giving the Terry Lectures in Yale (published as *The Structure of Religious Experience*) and the Deems Lectures in New York (revised and published as *The Boundaries of Science*). During the 1930s Macmurray also broadcast two series of lectures on BBC Radio, under the titles 'The Modern Dilemma' and 'Reality and Freedom' (collected and published as *Freedom in the Modern World*). It was around this time that Macmurray began to focus on publishing monographs. He had published a number of articles before this, but he had made a conscious decision not to write a book until he was forty years old, thereby giving his thoughts time to mature. The developing theme of personhood and the relations of persons permeate all of Macmurray's books and, within this, remnants of his early religious influences as well as his experiences of war come to the fore, primarily through the recurring themes of education, politics, fear and love.

When war broke out again, many of the staff and students from University College (UCL) relocated to Aberystwyth and Bangor, but Macmurray chose to remain in London (living in Jordans, a Quaker village in Buckinghamshire). Nevertheless, much of UCL, including Macmurray's office, was severely bombed during the London blitz, and he was forced to join the rest of the Philosophy department in Aberystwyth. With reduced student numbers, Macmurray had more time for research; thus, in keeping with his pre-war involvement with the Christian Left, he continued to produce work on democracy and socialism. In the early 1940s he insisted on returning to London to concentrate on the possibilities for Anglo-Soviet cooperation; it was around this time that he also gave a short series of BBC Radio Broadcasts called 'Persons and Functions'.

In 1944 Macmurray delivered the Upton Lectures on 'The Problem of Evil' at Manchester College, Oxford, before taking up the

Chair of Moral Philosophy in Edinburgh University. While he replaced A.E. Taylor in Edinburgh, Macmurray's vacated position in UCL was filled by A.J. Ayer. Macmurray's inaugural address had the title 'The Contemporary Function of Moral Philosophy', and in it he emphasized the need for moral philosophy to connect with everyday life and inform the relations of humans. Edinburgh afforded Macmurray the opportunity to become friends with Norman Kemp Smith and to serve later as Dean of the Faculty of Arts. It was also at Edinburgh University that Macmurray was instrumental in setting up the first British university course for nursing students, and he argued for a full nursing degree. His reputation as a lecturer grew and huge numbers of undergraduates attended his philosophy classes. In addition, he assisted Kenneth Barnes in the opening of the Wennington School, Lancashire, for holistic education, and he campaigned for the re-opening of the mature students college, Newbattle Abbey. During this time Macmurray gave the Dunning Lectures at Queen's University, Ontario (published as *The Conditions of Freedom*); he also lectured in the Gold Coast, Nigeria and Kenya, as part of his service on the Inter-University Council for Higher Education. Macmurray's most well-known lectures are the Gifford Lectures, which he delivered at Glasgow University in 1953 and 1954, where he was awarded an honorary LL.D. (The Giffords were given the title 'The Form of the Personal', and have been republished a number times as *The Self as Agent* and *Persons in Relation*.) Two years later, while still revising the Giffords for publication, Macmurray gave four BBC Radio talks entitled 'What Is Religion About?'. Then, in 1958, dissatisfied with the departmental move to amalgamate moral philosophy with logic and metaphysics, Macmurray took early retirement; he was sixty-seven years old.

For the first three months of his retirement, Macmurray toured the USA as the Danforth Visiting Lecturer. When he was back in the UK, he again took up residence in Jordans and, keen to find an undogmatic community with which to share his religious concerns, he applied for membership of the Society of Friends (Quakers). In the early 1960s Macmurray delivered the Forwood Lectures at Liverpool University (published as *Religion, Art and Science*), as well as recording another series of talks for BBC Radio, under the title 'To Save From Fear'. A few years after this, Macmurray's Gifford Lectures were published in paperback (perhaps the first Giffords to appear in this form), as well as being translated for a Spanish edition. Macmurray's health was deteriorating, but in 1970 he returned to Edinburgh to look after his mother; she died in 1973, at the age of 105. Then, on 21 June 1976, at the age of eighty five, Macmurray died. His wife, who survived him by six years, returned his ashes to Jordans.[1]

I: Dualism and its Solution

Macmurray's attempt to construct an adequate concept of the person begins with his attack on Descartes' famous phrase 'I think therefore I am'; or, rather, Macmurray attacks the dualism of mind and matter that lies behind Descartes' philosophy. While Cartesian philosophy identifies the human person with the mind, rather than the body, Macmurray claims that this is problematic, since it fails to make sense of our everyday experience of having both mind and body. As he states in our first extract, 'The Dualism of Mind and Matter':

> If I can properly say that I have a body and also that I have a mind, what is it that has them? If I am a mind, then that mind might perhaps have a body; and if I am a body then possibly that body might have a mind. But I cannot both be a body and have a body, nor can I be a mind and have a mind.[2]

Clearly Macmurray is only one of many to point out the problems inherent in Cartesian dualism; nevertheless, he contends that attempts to solve the problems have failed, because they still start from the standpoint of thought (and so presuppose mind–body dualism).

Alternatively, Macmurray suggests that we start from the standpoint of action, since action involves both mind and body. In our second extract, he examines the possibility of defining action, and concludes that philosophy which concentrates on reflective

---

[1]   A biography of Macmurray did not appear until 2002; see John E. Costello, *John Macmurray: A Biography* (Edinburgh: Floris Books, 2002). Macmurray's Swarthmore Lecture, published as *Search for Reality in Religion*, contains some autobiographical detail, as does the private collection of correspondence held by the John Macmurray Trust.

[2]   John Macmurray, 'The Dualism of Mind and Matter', *Philosophy*, 10 (1935), pp. 264–78, at p. 272.

activity is unable to offer a comprehensive definition. According to Macmurray, when we stop and think 'this negation of action is itself an action'.[3] In other words, thinking is one of the activities of humans — it is something we do. Hence, in the first volume of the Gifford Lectures, *The Self as Agent*, Macmurray states that: 'we should substitute the "I do" for the "I think" as our starting point and centre of reference'.[4] For Macmurray, therefore, rather than being primary as Descartes implies, thought is secondary to action. Even so, thought is regarded as being necessary; that is, the purpose of thinking is to increase our knowledge, enabling us to be more effective in action. Consequently, we are engaged in a necessary sequence — from action into reflection and back into action. This emphasis on action and the postulation of the 'self-as-agent' requires a fully worked-out account of action. In essence, Macmurray draws a distinction between acts and events, insisting that actions involve intentions, whereas events simply happen.

Furthermore, Macmurray argues that action, while informed by thought, is motivated by emotion. Thus, a concept of the person that unites mind and body also redresses the balance between reason and emotion. Macmurray is opposed to the view that emotion is chaotic and unruly and in need of suppression by reason. In this respect, Macmurray's work is ahead of its time; indeed, as contemporary psychology attests, the suppression of emotion is damaging to the development of the person. Nevertheless, Macmurray does not deny that emotion can be chaotic and unruly; however, he puts this down to a lack of education. We have a long history of educating the intellect, but the emotions have been seriously neglected. Hence, as with Aristotle, Macmurray argues for an emotional education, on the grounds that this will enable the emotions to be as reasonable as thought; that is, emotions can be appropriate to their object. As he states in our third extract: 'Reason is the capacity to behave consciously in

[3]   John Macmurray, 'What is Action?', *Proceedings of the Aristotelian Society*, supplementary volume 17 (1938), pp. 69–85, at p. 83.
[4]   John Macmurray, *The Self as Agent* (London: Faber, 1957; reprinted with an Introduction by Stanley M. Harrison, Atlantic Highlands, 1991; reissued, 1995), p. 84.

terms of the nature of what is not ourselves'.[5] Further, it is through our emotions that we grasp the intrinsic worth of objects; for example, to love someone is to value that person irrespective of his/her usefulness. As Macmurray puts it: 'The capacity to love objectively is the capacity which makes us persons'.[6] Consequently, if we are agents, as Macmurray maintains, we are more likely to be satisfied with our actions if we educate both the intellect and the emotions. An educated intellect will provide us with the means to achieve our intentions, and an education in the emotions will assist in the process of selecting worthwhile ends to pursue.

In essence, an emotional education amounts to training in sensibility — training in the ability to recognize different emotional responses and reactions to them, curbing reactions to inappropriate emotions and cultivating appropriate ones. Again, it is contemporary study that corroborates Macmurray's thesis; the work of Daniel Goleman, for example, reveals that success in adult life (in terms of contentment, motivation and the ability to establish long-term relationships) depends at least as much on emotional wisdom as it does on intellectual wisdom.

II: Early Relationships

Our initial emotional responses are learnt from our parents/carers, so understanding the development of human persons requires an examination of our earliest relationships. Macmurray only applies himself to this subject in his later work, as our fourth and fifth extracts reveal. In Macmurray's opinion, a fundamental aspect of personhood is the need, or the desire, to establish relations with other persons; this is demonstrated from birth. He states: 'the infant has a need which is not simply biological but personal, a need to be in touch with the mother, and in conscious perceptual relation with her'.[7] In other words, Macmurray refers to the relationship between the human infant and his/her pri-

[5]   John Macmurray, *Reason and Emotion* (London: Faber, 1935; reprinted with an Introduction by John E. Costello SJ, Atlantic Highlands, 1992; reissued, 1995), p. 7.
[6]   *Ibid.*, p. 15.
[7]   John Macmurray, *Persons in Relation* (London: Faber, 1961; reprinted with an Introduction by Frank G. Kirkpatrick, Atlantic Highlands, 1991; reissued, 1995), p. 49.

mary carer as a personal relationship, on the basis that both human infant and carer share an impulse to communicate with one another. Through communication the carer aims to teach the child to live as part of an interdependent community. Macmurray refers to the process through which this learning takes place as 'a rhythm of withdrawal and return'.[8] In order to encourage cooperation, the carer has to withdraw attention periodically. During the carer's absence, the child becomes fearful, and over a period of time this may turn into hatred for the carer. If this happens a loving relationship with the carer cannot be established, and, as the child grows to adulthood, future personal relationships may be affected. It is hoped, therefore, that the child will learn to wait patiently for the carer to return; if the child does this, a loving and positive relationship can continue.

III: Political Implications

Macmurray's analysis of personal relationships forces him to consider impersonal relations as well. In particular, he considers political and economic relations to be impersonal and is concerned with the extent that these assist or hamper personal relations. Hence, in our sixth extract Macmurray distinguishes between a 'substantival' and an 'adjectival' conception of society.[9] He describes the former as membership of a group, such as the State.

Our seventh extract, then, expands on Macmurray's view of the purpose of the State, which, he claims, is primarily to ensure justice through law. However, this in itself does not guarantee morality in our personal relations. Macmurray states: 'in the moral life justice is no all-inclusive obligation, but merely its basis and beginning'.[10] This claim is explained further in our eighth extract, where Macmurray argues that acting morally implies taking responsibility for our actions. That is, not acting so as to curtail the freedom of others, or, rather, not preventing them from acting

[8] *Ibid.*, p. 87.
[9] John Macmurray, 'The Conception of Society', *Proceedings of the Aristotelian Society*, 31 (1930–1), pp. 127–42, at p. 128.
[10] John Macmurray, 'Government by the People', *Journal of Philosophical Studies*, 2 (1927), pp. 532–43, at p. 543.

so as to realize their intentions.[11] In this piece Macmurray has both refined and clarified the distinction between types of societies, such that only the substantival conception is referred to as a society and the adjectival is called a community. Within a society people co-operate to achieve a specific purpose, so they are related to one another by virtue of their functions in the group — political parties and sports clubs are fitting examples here. While a society is a means to an end, then, a community is an end itself; people therein are related to one another as persons and not merely on the basis of their functions.

Much of Macmurray's work in the 1930s and 1940s is concerned with the relationship between societies and communities. In particular, he argues that the freedom and equality necessary for communities of friendship requires socialism rather than capitalism. While some of Macmurray's economic analysis seems dated now, his central argument is gaining credence; today, we might refer to this as a proper work–life balance. Macmurray is opposed both to the view that the personal life can be separated from the functional life and to the view that we live to serve society. On the contrary, in our ninth extract he states that: 'The functional life is *for* the personal life; the personal life is *through* the functional life'.[12] By this, he means that we work to live; we do not live to work. This principle is followed throughout his work on personal relationships, with the effect that his perception of morality is forward thinking. For example, when considering issues of sexual morality, Macmurray argues for emotional sincerity rather than monogamous marriage, on the grounds that institutions are there to serve us and not vice-versa.

IV: Religious Engagement

As contentious as this argument may appear to traditional Christianity, Macmurray does not abandon his religious heritage altogether. On the contrary, Macmurray insists that the creation and sustenance of community is a religious task, and, moreover, a

[11] See John Macmurray, 'Freedom in the Personal Nexus', in *Freedom: Its Meaning*, ed. Ruth N. Anshen (New York: Harcourt, 1940; London: Allen and Unwin, 1942), pp. 176–93, at p. 183.

[12] John Macmurray, 'Persons and Functions — 3: Two Lives in One', *The Listener*, 26 (1941), p. 822 (original italics).

Christian one. In this respect, it becomes clear that Macmurray
pre-dates the religiously plural society which we now live in,
since he does not offer a convincing argument concerning the effi-
cacy of Christianity, as compared with other religions, for engen-
dering community. Yet, he is highly critical of the individualism,
the otherworldliness and the doctrinal division found in
institutionalized Christianity. Alternatively, Macmurray suggests that being religious, and/or a Christian, means caring for
other persons and valuing ourselves. Hence, in our tenth extract
we find Macmurray arguing against the common Christian motif
of ultimate self-sacrifice — an area in which Macmurray's work is
proving useful to feminist theologians today — and in favour of
self-realization. He states: 'Self-realization is the true ideal of
human life, but it demands an understanding of the nature of the
self and its reality'.[13] In other words, as we have seen, human
nature is such that self-realization only comes about through
mutually reciprocated fellowship with other persons. According
to Macmurray, this insight is to be found in the reported life and
teachings of Jesus Christ. In the New Testament accounts, Jesus
chastises those who are fearful, advocating faith, love and forgiveness instead. Macmurray's interpretation of Jesus' life and
teaching is that fear and enmity hinder positive personal relationships, whereas faith in other persons, forgiveness and love enable
friendship. If this is Jesus' insight, it is not as unique as
Macmurray maintains, and yet it does give Jesus a significant
place alongside other visionaries and social activists, such as
Mahatma Gandhi and Martin Luther King.

In our eleventh extract, Macmurray sets out his view of religion
as a 'democratizing influence'[14] and a source of social cohesion.
Underlying Macmurray's assertion that religion promotes the
equality we need in order to be ourselves is the presumption that
religion has two key functions: 'the celebration of communion
and the creation of a universal family'.[15] Macmurray is not falling
into sentimentality and utopic dreams here; rather, he

[13] John Macmurray, 'Self-Realization', *The Expository Times*, 42 (1930),
     pp. 24–6, at p. 25.
[14] John Macmurray, 'What Is Religion About?- I', *The Listener*, 56 (1956),
     pp. 916–17, at p. 917.
[15] John Macmurray, 'What Is Religion About? — III', *The Listener*, 56 (1956),
     pp. 1027–8, at p. 1027.

emphasizes the important role that shared activities and rituals play in maintaining community spirit. In addition, he insists that a loving fellowship of persons does not exclude anyone on the grounds of race, class or sex; that is, it is based purely on common humanity and, therefore, it has the potential to include any and every person. Finally, in our twelfth extract Macmurray contends that, if there is such a thing as a Christian ethic, 'it is not thinkable in terms of duty and obligation';[16] it is an ethic of love. Again, it seems that there is nothing uniquely Christian about Macmurray's portrayal of what this means. Consequently, we can take advantage of this ambiguity and, in keeping with Macmurray's concerns, draw out the motif of inclusivity rather than any particular religious allegiance. Hence, the central tenets of Macmurray's thesis — the concept of the person and the ethics of personal relations — have much to offer in our present struggle with cultural and religious pluralism.

Esther McIntosh
Leeds, April 2004

---

[16]   John Macmurray, 'Prolegomena to a Christian Ethic', *Scottish Journal of Theology*, 9 (1956), pp. 1–13, at p. 3.

One

The Dualism of
Mind and Matter

I am willing to grant that all modern philosophy is dualistic and
that all the attempts to overcome this dualism have failed. But I
should give a very different account of the reasons for the failure. I
should maintain that any philosophy which starts by contrasting
Mind and Matter must necessarily fail to resolve the dualism
which its starting-point involves. I ask, therefore, why any philosophy should start from this contrast. Is there any real necessity for
thinking in terms of a dualism between Mind and Matter?

It may seem strange at first sight to say that the dualism of Mind
and Matter is characteristic of all modern philosophy. With the
qualified exception of the philosophy of Descartes, all the outstanding philosophical systems of modern times have been either
monistic or pluralistic. Berkeley's philosophy, with its thorough-
going denial of matter, is certainly not dualistic. It holds that the
only reality is mind and its activities, so that everything is mental.
But I had no intention to deny that most modern philosophical
systems are monistic in their conclusion as well as in their intention. What I wished to assert was that these monisms are all *in
terms of* the dualism of Mind and Matter. They start from the
hypothesis of a *prima facie* contrast between the mental and the
material, and reach their conclusion by unifying, in some way or
other, the two sides of the dualism which they take as *prima facie*
given. These philosophies could never arise except on the basis of
dualism. The dualism forms the primary hypothesis which they

[1]   From 'The Dualism of Mind and Matter', *Philosophy*, 10 (1935),
      pp. 264–78.

set out to examine. They discover, by critical analysis, that this dualism raises insuperable difficulties which force them to attempt its resolution. The final denial of dualism is still the result of thinking in terms of dualism. Berkeley's philosophy, for example, is obviously founded, in this sense, on the dualism of Mind and Matter. Without that distinction it could never get started. Berkeley begins by examining the idea of a two-substance world and goes on to show that all the things which we usually put in the basket labelled 'Material Substance' should really be put in the basket labelled 'Mental Substance'. In the structure of his thought there are still two classes, mental and material. But one of the classes turns out to be a null class. All the actual things in the world go into the mental class. When Berkeley says that everything is idea, the meaning of his statement depends upon the contrast that we draw between *ideas*, which are mental, and *things*, which are material. If Berkeley and his readers were not equally thinking in terms of a significant distinction between mind and matter, Berkeley's conclusion would itself carry no meaning at all. Thus apart from the dualistic habit of thought Berkeley's philosophy would never have come into existence, and could not be understood if it had. The same is true of all the classical modern philosophies. Even in their rejection of dualism they depend upon dualistic thinking. My question is this: 'Is there any rational justification for thinking dualistically?'

Our question, then, is not whether Reality is ultimately dualistic, but whether there is a *prima facie* case for suggesting that it may be; whether, that is to say, our common knowledge of the world suggests that a systematic attempt to understand it might naturally start by distinguishing two classes of things which seem at first sight to have nothing in common. Further investigation might then either confirm the dualism and so reach a dualistic conclusion or it might discover a way of resolving the dualism. But neither of these types of conclusion would arise unless there was a *prima facie* case for starting with a dualistic classification. Now a dualism, in the philosophical sense, is a metaphysical classification, a schema for dividing everything without exception into two sorts of things that have nothing in common, and which, therefore, exclude one another in their essential nature. If we consider that Reality may possibly be dualistic, we are considering that possibility that everything in Reality is either of one kind or of another, and that these two kinds have nothing in common and must be defined as mutually exclusive. If, for example, the dualism we are considering is the Mind–Matter dualism, then we are considering the possibility that everything in the Universe is either mental or material, and that nothing is both. We are considering that whatever is mental has none of the characteristics that belong to material things, and that nothing that is material possesses any of the characteristics that belong to mental things. A metaphysical dualism is, thus, both ultimate and absolute.

The history of modern philosophy shows that there is a deeply-rooted tendency in our minds to classify the constituents of Reality in this way. It also shows that such a dualistic classification raises great difficulties for the philosopher. It may be, of course, that no philosopher has yet hit upon the way to surmount those difficulties, and that we ought to go on making the attempt in the hope that we may finally be successful. But it may also be that the difficulties are of our own making, and that they really arise from the fact that the dualistic classification is merely an irrational tendency which we should attempt to overcome. It is between these two possibilities that we have to make our choice. That is why it is necessary to ask what are the *prima facie* grounds for starting out with the hypothesis that Reality divides without remainder into what is mental and what is material.

Let us first appeal directly to common sense, that is to say, to our ordinary unphilosophical outlook upon the world. The question that we shall then ask ourselves is: 'What kinds of things are there in the world as we know it which seem to be fundamentally different?' And the answer to that question would provide us with a natural *prima facie* classification of Reality. We shall begin (shall we not?) by distinguishing animate from inanimate things. This difference between things that are alive and things that are not alive is *prima facie* the obvious one. Whether it is ultimate or not is a different question, but not one with which we are now concerned. We shall then distinguish human beings, like ourselves, from both these classes. The main difficulty that we are likely to find will be in deciding whether to distinguish plant life from animal life. But on the whole we shall decide that this is really a subdivision of the class of animate but non-human things.

It might be possible to argue for a different natural classification, but hardly without sophistication. The division of the contents of the world into inorganic, organic, and personal seems at least to be a universal one and to correspond to what we can discover about the development of the human being in childhood. One thing is quite certain. We should never dream of dividing the things that we know into material things and mental things. It requires, at least, a high degree of sophisticated reflection to arrive at that classification. It is obviously not a natural classification of the contents of the world in comparison with the division into inanimate, animate, and rational or personal. This brings to light the first *prima facie* difficulty of the Mind–Matter dualism. It is difficult to find in it any place for living things that have no minds. If the world consists exclusively of mental things and material things, where do cabbages come in?

There is one quite simple consideration that reinforces this natural threefold classification against the dualism of Mind and Matter. Suppose that in spite of its unnaturalness, there is some deeper reason for classifying real things as either material or mental. We should expect that the systematic effort to investigate the nature of the world would result in the development of two separate lines of inquiry. We should expect to find the results of the investigation grouping themselves into two sciences or two groups of sciences, one having material things as its field of research and the other mental things. We should expect to find a set of physical sciences concerned with the investigation of matter and a set of psychological sciences concerned with the investigation of mind. Actually this was the expectation entertained by philosophers and scientists at the beginning of the scientific period under the influence of the dualistic habit of thought. Persistent efforts were made to develop two sciences concerned respectively with Mind and Matter. But the attempt has proved unavailing. The necessities of scientific development have forced another classification upon us, in spite of our prejudice in favour of dualism. We find ourselves with a set of physical sciences which are concerned with material phenomena. We find a set of sciences dealing with the phenomena of life, quite distinct from the physical sciences, but not concerned with mind at all. Finally, we find a special set of sciences, still rather unsure of themselves, which are concerned with psychological phenomena. In other words, the development of science reflects the natural threefold classification of reality and not the dualistic one, in spite of the fact that the dualistic tendency has exercised a continuous pressure upon the development of scientific investigation.

At first sight we might be inclined to draw the conclusion that the dualism of Mind and Matter was not exhaustive, and that what is required is the introduction of a third division into the classification. Instead of the twofold division into Matter and Mind, we might adopt a threefold division into Mind, Life, and Matter. Then we should look upon physical science as the science of Matter. Biological science as the science of Life, and Psychological science as the science of Mind. To do this would be to miss the point. Biology is not the science of Life, and Psychology is not the science of Mind in the sense that Physics is the science of Matter. Biology does not study Life in distinction from Matter. It studies the behaviour of living things, and living things are certainly material objects in some sense. Indeed, many biologists are of the opinion (wrongly, I believe), that as time goes on the biological sciences will become a special branch of physical science. As for Psychology, it is a commonplace of its history that it failed completely to develop so long as it was conceived as a science of Mind and that it has only achieved its recent qualified successes by deliberately abandoning this attempt and becoming a science of the behaviour of conscious beings and in particular of human beings. The importance of this lies in the fact that whatever a human being in the psychological sense may be, he is certainly not a mental constituent of Reality. In some sense he is just as much a material object as a brick or a penny whistle. Thus the appeal to common sense draws a blank. The natural outlook upon the world provides us with no *prima facie* ground for classifying the constituents of reality into mental and material. Indeed, it suggests a different classification which is incompatible with the dualism.

I imagine that anyone who is at all familiar with modern philosophy might be inclined to retort that everyone knows that the grounds for the Mind-Matter dualism arise in another field altogether, and that I have been deliberately wasting time. Before turning to consider the field in which the ground for the dualism is supposed to lie, I should like to justify my appeal to common sense. If the dualism of Mind and Matter is to have a real *prima facie* basis, the field which we have been considering is the field in which it *ought* to arise. If it does not arise naturally from the straightforward attempt to classify the kinds of things — the specifically different natures — to be found in the world, then that is in itself evidence that there is something wrong with it. For any metaphysical dualism offers itself as a classification, exhaustive and ultimate of the constituents of Reality. If experience shows that it is not possible to organize the detailed investigation of Reality on the basis of this classification, that is strong empirical evidence that the classification is a bad one. Philosophy, like any other systematic inquiry, must start with a classification; and since there is no other way of making a preliminary classification than by an appeal to the obvious and noticeable distinctions in the field of study, philosophy ought to start from the natural classification which common sense provides, especially when that classification is reinforced by the grouping of the sciences which are concerned with the investigation of special parts of the same general field. Indeed, the field to which we must now turn and in which the supposed grounds for the dualism are to be found, is itself the product of the dualistic tendency and presupposes it.

The centre of this field is determined by the perfectly natural and legitimate question, 'What am I?'. For some reason or other, traditional philosophy does not like to ask this question in its natural form. It prefers to ask, 'What is the Self?'. This is not, in fact, the same question. It is quite possibly a meaningless question. It is quite certain that I exist, that there is *me*. It is equally certain I submit, that there is *you*. But is there such a thing at all as *the Self*? If there is, it must be something which is as much me as it is you, and therefore, I should have thought, it can be neither you nor me. So I prefer to stick to the natural question, 'What am I?'. Of course it is mainly in connexion with the Theory of Knowledge that the suggestion of the dualism of Mind and Matter has arisen. But that question is really only a part of the wider question, 'What am I?' and it is worth our while to consider the wider question first before coming to that aspect of it which is concerned with our knowledge. Perhaps we can agree in general that the idea of dualism only arises when we consider our own nature. When we contrast Mind and Matter, we are primarily thinking about certain characteristics which belong to ourselves and to beings like ourselves, and which we are inclined to deny to other things in the world, even to animals. Thus it is only in reference to persons that the dualism arises at all, and persons form a relatively small class of objects in the world as we know it. That in itself suggests that the dualism is not really a metaphysical one but rather a personal one. It is a distinction within one of the natural classes into which common sense divides the constituents of Reality. But let us put this aside, and ask ourselves what it is about persons that suggests a dualism of Mind and Matter? In the first place, they are material objects, at least they have all the characteristics which we usually associate with material objects. They have size and shape and weight and so forth. Incidentally, we should notice that they have all the characteristics of animate things as well. They grow and they reproduce their species. Even within the special class of persons our natural threefold classification insists on reappearing. But they have certain special characteristics which set them in a class apart. They have special ways of behaviour which do not seem to be covered by our ordinary conceptions of what material objects or living creatures are. We need not trouble ourselves at the moment to define or even to enumerate these special characteristics. We need only notice that people cannot be understood or investigated in the same way and through the same conceptions as material objects or even as living organisms, without leaving out something that is of the essence of their nature. Or, to put it more simply and more fundamentally, we cannot deal with people in the way in which we can deal with other things, without frustrating our own efforts and failing in our intentions. But in all this there is no suggestion of a dualism of Mind and Matter.

Indeed, the dualism would never suggest itself but for one fact, that we ourselves, who are carrying on the investigation, belong to this class of things, and that our knowledge of ourselves is very different from our knowledge of other people like ourselves. I know myself from inside, as it were, while I know other people only from outside. I know myself as a set of activities and energies to which I give the general name of consciousness. But I also know myself from outside in the same way as I know you, though not so well. It is worth while to remember that our external knowledge of ourselves is not so complete or satisfactory as our external knowledge of other people. But there is enough of it, perhaps, to enable it to act as a kind of middle term between our knowledge of ourselves and of them. It suggests to us that other people know themselves as we know ourselves, from inside, and that they know us as we know them, from outside. I do not wish to endorse this as an account of how we come to know other persons as persons, but it is certainly a natural account and true so far as it goes. It indicates, however, how we come to think of ourselves in a dual way, as known from outside and from inside, or to put it in terms of the dualism, from the mental side and from the material side. Here, then, for the first time we come across a fact that seems to suggest a dualism between Mind and Matter so far as persons are concerned. It is not, I believe, the real root of the dualistic illusion, because the formulation of it as a distinction between mental and material aspects, presupposes that we have already adopted the Mind–Matter dualism as a basis of our classification. But we may let that pass for the moment.

Now, if we admit that this suggests a dualism, we must notice that it is not the metaphysical dualism of Mind and Matter. It could only lead us to credit the class of things that we call persons with a dual nature. At most it would suggest that persons consist of a body and a mind, and that these two constituents, as we experience them, are radically different and mutually exclusive. It may be psychologically natural to read this dualism into the nature of Reality as a whole. To do so would be a form of anthropomorphism, for it would consist in projecting what we take to be a characteristic of human beings into the field of objective Reality. The tendency to anthropomorphism, however, does not constitute a good reason for accepting the dualism of Mind and Matter as a metaphysical classification.

But is there any ground for thinking that the double way in which we are aware of ourselves suggests a dualism of mind and body as the proper analysis of persons? It arises only for each of us in one particular case, our own. If we were to forget ourselves and to think only of our experience of other people, we should conclude that they were living beings with certain special peculiarities of behaviour. There would be no *prima facie* suggestion that what we know when we know another person is some combination of a body and a mind. In other words, unless we had already accepted the dualistic classification of persons, we should never use it to interpret our experience of other persons. The dualism of body and mind could only arise through a reflection upon the two ways in which I am aware of myself, through external perception and through introspection. In this case, it is suggested that we are aware of our bodies in external perception and of our minds in introspection.

But are we? Let us examine the inference that is involved. The premiss which we take from our experience is the proposition, 'I know myself both from outside and from inside'. The conclusion is that 'I know my mind and I know my body'. It is surely impossible to infer the second from the first. The first implies that one and the same entity is known in two different ways. The second implies that two different entities are known in one and the same way. The transition is obviously illogical. If introspection is myself knowing a mind, and the external perception is myself knowing a body, then I can be neither the body nor the mind, nor *a fortiori* the two together. If I can properly say that I have a body and also that I have a mind, what is it that has them? If I am a mind, then that mind might perhaps have a body; and if I am a body then possibly that body might have a mind. But I cannot both be a body and have a body, nor can I be a mind and have a mind. Surely if it is true that I know myself in two distinct ways — and that seems incontrovertible — then I cannot consist of a mind and a body which are mutually exclusive. I can properly generalize my experience by saying that it is a characteristic of persons that they have the capacity of knowing themselves in two different ways. To introduce a Mind–Body dualism is to deny this. Therefore, this fact provides no logical grounds even for a dualism of mind and body.

I should like, in this connexion, to draw your attention to a fundamental difference between the dualism of mind and body and the dualism of Mind and Matter. When we distinguish between our minds and our bodies, we are thinking of our bodies not as material objects but as animal organisms. We are contrasting our rational with our animal nature. By body in this antithesis, we do not mean what the physicist means when he says 'all bodies gravitate', but when we use the Mind–Matter dualism this is precisely what we mean by 'matter'. Thus if we came to the conclusion that the Mind–Body dualism was a proper one, that would afford no logical ground for the Mind–Matter dualism. We could not logically pass from the one to the other. If we refer back to the natural threefold division of the constituents of the world into material objects, living beings, and persons, we can see that the Mind–Matter dualism arises, though illegitimately, through a contrast between the first and the third which omits the second, while the Mind–Body dualism arises, though again improperly, from the contrast of the second and third, which omits the first. That is why Descartes, for example, who started from the Mind–Matter dualism, was forced to consider all living beings, with the exception of persons, as automata.

We must now turn to the field in which the dualism of Mind and Matter has been most discussed in modern philosophy — the field of the Theory of Knowledge. If we reject, for philosophical purposes, our natural tendency to limit our thinking to the objective field of what we experience, leaving our experiencing of it out of account, and try to think of the total fact of ourselves experiencing the world, we have to take a new distinction into account. We have to distinguish between that which knows and that which is known, between the subject and the object. The logical dualism of subject and object describes the fundamental form of any cognitional experience whatever. In any case of knowing, there must be a subject — that which knows, and an object — that which is known. Logically, subject and object are correlative terms which exclude one another. By definition, the subject is that in any instance of knowing which is not the object; and that object is that which is not the subject. Now, in actual fact, it is we who know, and, therefore, it is natural to identify ourselves with the subject in experience. But also we use the term 'mind' as a generic term for that which knows, and, therefore, we tend to identify the subject with mind and so ourselves with instances of mind. This is, in fact, the normal way in which the dualism of Mind and Matter appears in modern philosophical discussions. 'I am a thinking being', says Descartes, 'that is to say, a knower. Mind, in general, is that which knows. Therefore, I am a mind'. In other words, the terms 'subject', 'mind', and 'self', or 'ego', or 'I' are all in different references definable as 'that which knows'. And as soon as mind is identified with the subject it is natural, where the dualistic tendency is already in operation, to identify matter with the object. It is natural, I say, although it is completely illogical. The connexion is purely an association of ideas. If we are operating with a distinction between Mind and Matter and also with a distinction between subject and object, and if there is in the field which we are investigating a ground for identifying the subject with mind, there will be a psychological tendency to identify the object with matter. Thus there is a psychological explanation ready to our hand for the association of the logical dualism of subject and object with the metaphysical dualism of Mind and Matter.

There is, however, no logical justification for this association. In the first place, a logical dualism is formal. A metaphysical dualism is not. A metaphysical distinction is a distinction *in the object*. It is part of the analysis of what is known, and has nothing therefore to do with a logical distinction between what knows and what is known. What knows from a metaphysical point of view is part of what is known, and is, therefore, considered as object. If there is a reason for identifying the subject with mind, there is absolutely none for identifying the object with matter. Indeed, the association at once denies the possibility of metaphysics or even psychology. For, unless mind can be the object in a case of knowing, there can obviously be no knowledge of mind, and if mind is a constituent of reality, there can then be no knowledge of Reality. But the identification of the object with matter is palpably grotesque, since no one who makes it ever means (as he ought to mean) that the only objects of knowledge are material ones. The dualism of Mind and Matter is, indeed, the belief that the world which we know — that is to say, the world as object — consists of two kind of objects, mental and material. To identify the object with matter implies, therefore, that the dualism of Mind and Matter is false, and logically must lead to a pure materialism in metaphysics. Any philosophy, therefore, which confuses the subject-object distinction with the Mind–Matter distinction, is inherently materialistic, however ideal may be the terminology in which it is expressed. The two distinctions have, in fact, no point of contact, and, therefore, the logical distinction between subject and object can never provide any reason for a belief in the dualism of Mind and Matter. Unless we already had the Mind–Matter dualism in our thoughts, the association of the two would never be set up. This in itself indicates that the source of the dualism of Mind and Matter cannot lie in the logical field.

There is another feature of the logical distinction which is, I believe, not usually appreciated, but which is very important for modern philosophy. It is that the distinction between subject and object, however essential it may be for logic, cannot be made the starting-point of any philosophical inquiry into the nature of Reality, because it cannot legitimately be generalized. When I begin to reflect upon my experience, I quite naturally draw a distinction between myself experiencing and what I experience. I have no objection to that distinction. It is quite a proper one. But it is a different distinction for each one of us. If I draw it, it puts me on one side of the line and everything else on the other. If you draw it, it puts you on one side of the line and everything else, including me, on the other. Each person is both subject and object; subject for himself and object for every other subject. If I try to use this distinction between myself and what I experience as the basis of a metaphysical construction (as Descartes did, for example) I imply that I am the only subject and that all other persons are parts of the object-world. I am, in the world, that which knows. Everybody else is part of what is known. I am, in fact, unwittingly committed to solipsism. Solipsism is the philosophical correlative of egoism or individualism. It corresponds to the practical attitude which says 'I am the only agent. The rest of the world is material for the service of my selfhood'. All individualist philosophy — that it to say, practically all modern philosophy — does illegitimately generalize the subject in order to escape the dilemma of solipsism. It does so by assuming that there are a large number of different 'I's', yet that all of them, in some mystical sense, are really the same 'I' repeated at different points in space and time. That is why it is driven to talk of *the* Ego or *the* Self or *the* Mind or, in another connexion, *the* Will. For, if the different subjects were really different, they would all have to be credited with different objects, and there would be no common world or Universe for them to discuss or to belong to. But because of its starting-point such philosophy can only produce a pluralism of solipsisms — a plurality of unrelated worlds — which is of course a blank absurdity. This point is so fundamental that it is difficult even to express it or to become aware of it, since we are all individualists with minds shaped by an individualistic tradition. But it shows itself in the fact that our modern philosophy completely ignores the second person. It is full of Ego and Meum, but it knows nothing of Tu and Tuum. Yet the terms 'I' and 'You' are strictly correlative, and their correlation is the proper truth in the familiar statement that human nature is essentially social. The 'I' in isolation is non-existent. The real unit of rational experience on the subject side is not 'I' but 'I and You', in mutual relation.

The logical distinction, then, between Subject and Object affords no ground for accepting or even considering a metaphysical dualism of Mind and Matter. To argue that since I am a subject aware of objects, therefore what I am aware of must be divided into material entities and mental entities, is a palpable *non sequitur* of the crudest kind. Is there, then, any other field in which we can hope to discover a *prima facie* ground for entertaining the idea of a dualism of mental and material? There is only one other direction, so far as I can see, in which we may look. It is the distinction between things and images. But before examining this distinction, which comes nearer to suggesting a dualism than any of the others, I should like to dispose of a purely verbal confusion that might tend to blur the argument at this point. All persons have certain capacities, such as thinking, remembering, perceiving, imagining, deciding, and so on, which we are accustomed to describe as *mental* capacities. I can see no objection to this use of the term *mental* so long as we do not read the Mind–Matter dualism into it. We should do this if we implied by the term 'mental capacities' that these were the powers of an entity called a 'mind'. The issue may become clearer if we compare an analogous case. We speak in a similar way of the 'vital' functions of organisms. They have such vital capacities as assimilating food and reproducing themselves. But no one imagines that this suggests that 'vital functions' means functions of something called 'life', which is somehow dualistically conjoined with the bodies of organisms. Why, then, should anyone think that the phrase 'mental capacities' means capacities of something called a mind. Surely only because they already have the dualism of Mind and Matter, or rather of Mind and Body in their thinking. This is indeed characteristic of most arguments advanced in favour of the dualism as well as of a great number (such a Berkeley's) which are raised against it. They are themselves consequences of dualistic thought, and can therefore neither support the dualism nor refute it. They presuppose it.

But the distinction of things and images, or, more satisfactorily, of things that exist and things that are imagined, is on a different footing. In some sense we must admit that there are hosts of things which, as we say, exist only in idea, or are purely imaginary. If, then, we are to begin our philosophical task with a classification of all that there is, must we not start with the distinction between two classes of objects, one class which exists independently and one which exists only 'in the mind'? And is not this distinction logically prior to what we called the 'natural' classification of things into inanimate, animate, and personal, since that is a classification which refers only to the things which exist independently? Surely here we have at least a *prima facie* case for the dualism of Mind and Matter?

I do not think that it provides even a *prima facie* suggestion of the dualism. The reason why it seems to do so is that we are apt to state the distinction, as I have just done, in terms which are the product of the dualism. If we talk of objects which exist in the mind and objects which exist independently of the mind, we are obviously assuming the existence of the mind as an entity and therefore we have assumed the dualism. Any conclusion in favour of the dualism which we draw from this premise will inevitably be circular and fallacious. We must first state the distinction in a form which does not assume the dualism. And this is not merely possible, it is the natural way to state it. For common sense the distinction is one between imaginary things and real things. The unicorn, for example, is an imaginary animal, while the horse is a real animal. In this form the distinction offers no *prima facie* ground for dualism; indeed it implies the opposite. For the dualism is a classification of Reality into its real components, while the distinction between real and imaginary things excludes the latter from Reality and implies that they do not exist in Reality and cannot therefore be constituents of it.

But we cannot leave the matter here, because someone will at once object that imaginary objects are part of our experience and that we cannot therefore merely ignore them in a philosophical account of the nature of things. That is of course true, and we must agree that a philosophy which took no account of the imagination and its activities would be ridiculous. But the question is only whether the facts necessitate a dualistic interpretation from the beginning. Now there is one peculiar difficulty which will arise if we answer this question in the affirmative. If we divide the whole of what we experience into imaginary entities and real entities, and insist that this implies a dualism of Mind and Matter, on which side of the dualism will mind fall? Is my mind an 'imaginary' or a 'real' entity? If we answer that it is not an imaginary entity we shall have to conclude that every actual mind is a material entity; and that makes nonsense of the dualism. If we reply that mind is an imaginary entity — and that is in my opinion the proper answer — then we must assume that I imagine it, and that I am not an imaginary entity, but a real one; and therefore, in terms of the dualism, that I am a material entity.

Now, common sense maintains that *we produce* the objects of our imagination, and that therefore they depend on us for their existence. Their existence *is* their being imagined. But there is a stream of philosophical tradition which establishes another type of dualism by an implicit denial of this dependence of what is imagined on the person who imagines it. Why, it may be asked, should the objects we imagine (or to use an old phrase of Plato's, who is the main source of this thought), the objects we can only see with the eye of the soul, be more dependent upon us for their existence than the objects we perceive with our bodily senses? This may be taken in either of two ways. We may answer either that what we perceive and what we imagine are equally independent. The first gives us the Platonic metaphysic with its dualism of two worlds, both independent of the persons who apprehend them; the second gives us modern Idealism in which both real objects and imaginary objects are considered to be equally mind-dependent. But the idealist solution presupposes the Mind–Matter dualism and so does not concern us now; while the Platonic dualism can find no place for the person who both perceives and imagines. He cannot be properly assigned to either of the two worlds and can only be included in the classification at all by the *tour de force* of supposing that he belongs to both at once.

To suppose this is to suppose that the same entity is at once real and imaginary.

We must return, then, to our proper question, whether the distinction between real and imaginary objects provides a *prima facie* case for the dualism of Mind and Matter. Since it is a *prima facie* case that we are seeking, we must accept the *prima facie* dependence of imagined objects upon the person who imagines them. Now this provides a *prima facie* case against the dualism, unless we are prepared to make the ridiculous assumption that 'I depend upon the activities of my own mind for my existence'. The objects which I imagine, so far as they are imaginary objects, and not real objects apprehended through imagination, are functions of my imagining and dependent upon me. I myself am a real object, not an imaginary one whether I am aware of myself from without or from within. I recall here this dual self-awareness in order to emphasize the point that in introspection it is *myself* that is apprehended. If, therefore, I am aware through introspection of images or 'objects of imagination', I am aware of them as dependent on me, as modifications of my own real nature. These images and ideas, then, if they are in any sense constituent parts of reality, can only be so because they are constituent parts of me. They can be elements in Reality only because I am an element in reality, and not in their own right. I can only contrast them with the rest of Reality by contrasting myself with the rest of Reality. The question about the nature of images is thus part of the question about the nature of persons, and it falls within the natural classification of Reality into inanimate things, living organisms, and persons. It follows that the distinction between things and images cannot provide a *prima facie* case in favour of a dualism of Mind and Matter. At the most it can be construed, and, illegitimately construed, in terms of the dualism, if the dualism has already been presupposed.

The effort to construe the distinction between imaginary entities and real entities as a dualism of Mind and Matter has a very curious corollary which may well form the conclusion of this essay. If by 'my mind' I mean the complex of entities which are revealed by introspection, in contrast to the objects which are revealed by the bodily senses, then 'my mind' must be a complex imaginary object. Now the characteristic of any imaginary object or mental entity lies in the fact that its 'esse' is 'imaginari'. It exists, that is to say, only in and through the activity which apprehends it. If, then, I cease to think or imagine 'my mind', it ceases to exist. If we all were to cease thinking that there is such a thing as mind, there would cease to be such a thing as mind. If, on the other hand, I mean by 'my mind' my activities of thinking and perceiving and imagining and so on, if I mean, that is to say, 'me thinking', then I am a real entity possessed of these capacities, and there is no need to suppose that I must have a mind in order to possess them. For common sense at least, the 'I' that thinks — certainly the 'you' that thinks — is an object that can be seen and heard and handled.

I cannot claim that this search for a reason for entertaining the dualism of Mind and Matter is exhaustive. There may be a field which has been overlooked. But it seems to me to reveal such egregious implications of that dualism as to justify a highly sceptical attitude, and to suggest the effort to describe the nature of Reality without assuming a dualistic classification as the proper starting point of any new philosophical construction. The proper supplement of this essay would be an explanation of how the dualistic illusion arises. Such an inquiry, however, falls within the province of the psychologist rather than of the philosopher.

Two

What is Action?

I wish to raise the question 'What is action?' in the sense in which it is the primary question of Ethics and of any other branch of practical philosophy. I do so as the result of a growing conviction that it has never been formulated or discussed by philosophers; and that until this is done, all practical philosophy must be based upon uncriticized and even unrecognized assumptions. To this I should add that in the last analysis the question is just as fundamental to every branch of theoretical philosophy, because thinking is, in some sense, action, even if it is normally contrasted with action. Thinking is one of the things we *do*.

When Descartes defined man as a thinking substance in the 'Cogito, ergo sum', he distinguished between the activity of thinking and its products, without becoming fully aware of the implications of so doing. The effect of this has been to shift the emphasis in philosophy from the objects of knowledge to the activities of knowing. The modern concern with methodology is one symptom of this. It is one of Kant's greatest claims to a supreme place in the history of philosophy that he did realize, more fully than any other, what these implications are. He did not doubt the claims of traditional logic to be an exact and a priori science. But he realized that its investigation of thought was limited to the products of thinking, and that there was a need to raise the question about the forms of the activity of thinking. The nature of the spontaneity of the mind in the search for knowledge has remained, ever since, the central question of modern philosophy; and any philosopher who sought to return to the older dogmatic assumptions, disregarding the problem raised by the recognition

[1]   From 'What is Action?', *Proceedings of the Aristotelian Society*, suppl. 17 (1938), pp. 69–85.

that the mind does something in the production of knowledge, and is not merely receptive, would rightly be counted naïve.

But in Ethics no similar recognition has appeared, and the neglect of Ethics in general, and its intellectual problems, may not be unconnected with this. Our practical philosophy persists in its analysis of acts, or of our judgments about action, without seeing that what is first required is an examination of action. Acts are, I take it, the products of the external manifestations of action. They are the observable changes in the world which we habitually refer, for their origin, to the desires and intentions of human beings. They are *what we do*. Behind this objective consideration of acts lies the unanswered question 'What is *doing*?'. What is the unobservable subjective side, as it were, of the process of which these observable acts are the objective expression? Alternatively, moralists have concentrated on the question of right and wrong, seeking to discover which acts or classes of acts are right and which are wrong; or, more subtly, with Kant, they have asked, 'How do I act when I act rightly?'. Yet it seems that all such questions and investigations presuppose that we know what action is, that we accept it as given and understood and that our knowledge of action is such that no questions about it need be asked. Those philosophers who have clearly realized that in the theoretical field a theory of knowledge is required have not recognized a similar need for a theory of action in the ethical field. They have recognized the 'I think' that accompanies all my judgments. They have not recognized the 'I do' that accompanies all my activities, including my activity of thinking. It is this most fundamental of all questions which I wish to raise. I do not propose to attempt to answer it. I shall be content if I can make it clear what the question is and suggest one or two lines of consideration which may help to reveal its importance, and the poverty of our resources for dealing with it.

From the grammarian's point of view action is that which is expressed by verbs. The distinction between substantives and verbs is the most fundamental distinction in the field of language. The substantive is primarily the linguistic form which denotes an object. This at least suggests that the distinction between *object* and *action* is a fundamental distinction in reality. How otherwise could the necessity for a grammatical distinction between substantives and verbs be accounted for? And if this is so, any conception of action which assimilates it to the conception of an object, and any analysis of action which treats it as if it were an object, must ignore or at least misrepresent the nature of action. Further, the characterization of objects and actions is achieved differently by language. Substantives are qualified by adjectives. Verbs are modified by adverbs. This again suggests that we may go badly astray if we assume that the distinction between adjectives and adverbs is logically unimportant. If we may say, with some logicians, that the properties of an object are 'adjectival' to it, we ought to maintain the distinction between object and action by saying that the modalities — not the properties — of an action are 'adverbial' to it. The grammatical need to distinguish between adjectival and adverbial relation seems to indicate that there is an underlying ground in reality for distinguishing two types of characterization, one which is appropriate to what is expressed by the verb — viz., action; and another which is appropriate to what is expressed by the substantive — viz., the object. We must beware, therefore, of assuming that the substitution of the substantive-adjective form for the verb–adverb form of expression in our enquiries into the modalities of action is safely admissible. It is likely to misrepresent the character of that which we are attempting to describe or analyse.

The bearing of this upon our ethical studies is obvious. Modern ethics is accustomed to examine statements of the form 'This action is good' or 'This action is right'. Such statements refer to action by means of substantives and to the ethical modalities of action by means of adjectives. Action then appears to be an object and its characters appear to be qualities or properties of the object, 'adjectival' to it. Some thinkers have insisted that the first question which the ethical philosopher must answer concerns the meaning of 'good', and in a way which suggests, to my mind at least, that they assume that the adjective 'good' refers to a property of certain 'objects' in reality. I do not see how any enquiry which begins by examining propositions of the form 'X is good' can well do otherwise. Yet the consideration of the linguistic necessity of distinguishing verbs from substantives and adverbs from adjectives throws grave doubt upon any such procedure. The natural form in which to express moral judgments is rather 'X acted rightly' or 'X did well'. I suggest that it is essential for ethical philosophy to accept such forms as the proper forms of statement, and to conduct its analysis accordingly.

But here we find a seemingly insuperable obstacle. The available methods of logical analysis do not provide us with the means to do so. Our first exercises in traditional logic are designed to teach us to put propositions into logical form. Language, we are rightly told, has a double use. It is employed to convey information, but also to express feeling and emotion. For logical purposes this second use of language must be eliminated. Unfortunately the actual process of logical reformulation gets rid of a good deal more than the emotive element in expression. It loses the verbal and adverbial forms also. Traditional logic retains only the verb 'to be', limiting it to the present tense. The only modifications allowed are those of person and number, which are dictated by the grammatical subject. It then ceases to function as a verb in any real sense, and becomes a 'copula' denoting the relation between logical subject and logical predicate — the symbol of predication. There have been debates on the question of whether the copula expresses existence, but none that I have come across on the question of whether it expresses action. Modern improvements in logic have enlarged its scope as an instrument of analysis very greatly. But they have done nothing to help us in this particular dilemma. Indeed, contemporary logic has got rid of the last vestige of the verbal form and substituted the idea of a relation between terms which are substantival or adjectival in character.

What justification have we for this exclusion of verbs, with their apparatus of moods, tenses and voices and their adverbial modifications from the recognized forms of logical statement? It has clearly nothing to do with the emotive functions of language. Indeed, in statements about action the substitution of the traditional 'logical' form for the natural verbal form is one of the common devices for heightening emotional effect. 'Albert's table manners are disgusting' is a more highly emotive form of expression than 'Albert behaves disgustingly at table'. The verbal forms of statement are means of expressing knowledge and conveying pure information. They form the basis of inferences just as certainly as the substantival forms. Such inferences are typical of legal arguments. If a murder has been committed at the house of

the accused and the following two propositions can be established for the defence:

(a)   that fifteen minutes before the crime was committed the
       accused left his place of business and walked all the way
       home

(b)   that no man can cover the distance between the accused's
       place of business and his home on foot in less than twenty
       minutes

then it has been demonstrated logically that the accused is not
guilty of the murder. Such inferences depend upon the expression of our knowledge of action by means of verbs. Yet I know of
no recognized logical form into which such propositions can be
cast without doing intolerable violence to their logical content.
What is the proper logical analysis of such statements as 'The
party on the ice-field trudged laboriously southwards', or 'He
glared furiously at his opponent'?

Now a logical schema is in some sense a form of thought not
merely a form of language. So far as it is concerned with language
it is concerned to determine the proper forms of linguistic expression for the purposes of thinking. Any attempt to think of the
world through logical forms which do not recognize verbs and
their modifications runs the risk of failing to express action altogether. That in our knowledge of the world which requires verbs
and adverbs for its expression will remain unexpressed. There is a
danger that the conceptual representation of the world which
such a logic necessitates will imply that all action is unreal; or, in
other words, that there is no such thing as action.

The term 'action' is involved in the same ambiguity that recent
philosophy has found it essential to resolve in the case of terms
like 'perception' or 'conception'. It may refer either to what is
done, or to the doing of it. It may mean either 'doing' or 'deed'.
When we talk of 'an action' we are normally referring to what is
done. When we talk of turning from thought to action, the reference, on the contrary, is to a change in the mode of the Self's activity. The Self ceases to behave as a Subject and behaves instead as
an Agent. The important question about action is that question
which is concerned, not with the characters of what is done, but
with the nature of acting. The question 'What is action?' must
therefore be resolved into two questions, viz., 'What is acting?'

and 'What is an act?'. If we make this necessary distinction, it carries with it a further question concerning he relation between 'acting' and 'act', upon which I propose at once to make the following comment. If the parallel distinction is made into the case of 'perception', it has to be conceded that there is no inherent necessity to believe that what is perceived depends for its existence upon the perceiving of it. But this is not so in the case of action. In this case it is inherent in the very notion of action that what is done depends for its existence on the doing of it. To act is to effect a change in the external world. The deed is the change so effected. What is done is, by definition, not in the mind, but in the world of existence and it has consequences in the world of existence which are not under the control of the mind. Repentance, as the moralist reminds us, cannot cancel the consequences of our actions, though new actions may modify them. Action proceeds from the Self to the world. It terminates in things, not in ideas. What is done, in action, would not be at all but for the doing of it. It might seem at first sight possible to maintain that the change in the world which is the deed depends upon the doing of it only for being a deed, not for being a change *in rerum natura*. The tree that is pulled down by a tempest. But reflection shows that this is not the case. Action, because it terminates in the objective world, is inherently particular. What is done is necessarily this particular act. No doubt similar changes might occur which are not deeds, but natural happenings. But the deed which is the uprooting of this particular tree at this particular time under those particular conditions is dependent for its occurrence on human action. Apart from the acting this particular change would not have occurred. And there are changes in the world which could not take place apart from action, such as the building of a cathedral or the construction of a typewriter. The dependence of the deed on the doing of it is in the full sense an existential dependence, and this is involved in the definition of action.

The implications of this dependence of the act upon the doing of it are far-reaching. It follows that any analysis of action which represents the activity of the Self in action and the change in the objective world as 'externally' related to one another will misrepresent the character of action. An analysis, for example, which represents action as consisting of two events, one mental, the other material, with a *de facto* relation between them, is not merely inadequate; it implies that there is no such thing as action. For it implies that it is possible to think the existential independence of what is done from the doing of it, to conceive the deed as not a deed but an occurrence. Any philosophy which seeks to analyse action in terms of a distinction between subjective and objective; any philosophy which conceives the Self as a Mind, or defines the Self as a Subject, must be incapable of giving a true account of action. The distinction between the subjective and the objective is, it should be remembered, a subjective distinction. It signalizes, indeed, the withdrawal of the Self from action into reflection, and the adoption of an attitude of contemplation in relation to the external world. The Self as Subject is the Self as knower and not agent. If the distinction between Subject and Object is taken objectively, it becomes a distinction between two kinds of objects, and gives rise to the dualism of mind and matter, of mental events and material events, or to the body–mind problem. As a consequence, we must analyse any action into a mental occurrence (usually called an act of will) and a physical event, of which the primary component is a movement of the Agent's body. The relation that is presumed to hold between these two events is confessedly a mystery. But even if it could be satisfactorily defined the real difficulty would not be removed. Neither of the two events so distinguished is an action. The determination of a relation between them does not improve matters. Two events necessarily related may perhaps constitute a causal sequence. They assuredly do not constitute an action. An action is not the concomitance of an intention in the mind and an occurrence in the physical world; it is the *producing* of the occurrence by the Self, the *making* of a change in the external world, the *doing* of a deed. No process which terminates in the mind, such as forming an intention, deciding to act, or willing, is either an action or a component of action. In certain circumstances such a mental event or process may be followed *necessarily* by action. But the fact that it can be followed by action is itself enough to show that it is neither action nor a component of action. The analysis of the idea of action does not deal with the concomitants of action, but with action itself; and it yields only the distinction between the *doing* and the *deed*. It may be convenient to refer to these two aspects of action by the Latin words which distinguish them — *actio* and *actum*.

What then is *action*? What is 'acting'? It is contrasted with *cogitatio* or thinking. The *prima facie* contrast might be stated by saying that we can either *act* or *think*, or that when we are thinking we are not acting and when we are acting we are not thinking. If a friend finds me in my study by the fire, where I have been trying to sort out my ideas, and asks me what I have been doing, I may reply 'Nothing at all, only thinking'. This common way of speaking marks the limitation of the idea of acting to those of my activities in which I operate upon the not self and produce changes in the material world. In thinking, on the other hand, my activity is directed inwards upon my own consciousness and operates upon ideas. The question of whether I can, as a matter of fact, both think and act at the same time is, I suppose, strictly irrelevant to the issue. But it suggests two points which are instructive. In the first place, it is difficult, if not impossible, to think and act at the same time, unless one or the other form of activity is relatively automatic. The more concentration a particular activity of thought requires the more action tends to be inhibited. And if a particular action is difficult to perform, its performance becomes incompatible with thinking. If we must think we have to stop work to do it. There is therefore a *de facto* tendency for thinking and acting to inhibit one another. This contrast tends to be obscured in modern philosophy by a tendency to use the term 'thinking' as equivalent to, or at least as inclusive of, 'being aware', or 'being conscious' or 'knowing'. It gives rise to a tendency to contrast acting with knowing, or even with consciousness. But this is patently a mistake. The Self is just as conscious in action as in thought, and we know when we are acting at least as certainly — perhaps more certainly — than when we are thinking. Consciousness and knowledge characterize the Self in all its behaviour. Thinking and acting are contrasted and to some extent incompatible modes of its behaviour.

But the question is not, after all, a question of fact. Facts are involved, of course; but the essential distinction between thinking and acting lies in the direction of intention; and a matter of intention is not a matter of fact. Thinking is a mode of the Self's activity which intends a modification of consciousness; while acting intends a modification of the world. This reference to intention is specially important in dealing with those cases in which action and thought are interwoven and involve one another. The reason why we rightly include scientific experiment in the theoretical field is that it is part of a total activity of the self which intends knowledge. The small boy who is discovered at work on the kitchen clock with a screwdriver replies, therefore, with some justice, to the accusation that he is breaking the clock, that he is *not* breaking it, he is finding out how it works. In such cases the action involved is accidental to the activity of thinking. Similarly, a change in consciousness which is involved in our acting upon the world is accidental to that mode of the Self's activity, since the form of activity is defined by its intention. For this reason we do not include the elaboration of technical rules in a general theory of knowledge.

Actio is, then, one of the two modes of the activity of a self. It is contrasted with *cogitatio* by the direction of its intention. In acting, the Self appears as an Agent seeking to effect changes in the world; in thinking, it appears as a knower seeking to effect changes in our consciousness of the world. The question of the relation of these two modes is a difficult one which cannot be entered upon now. But we might note in passing that there is *prima facie* evidence that *actio* is primary and *cogitatio* secondary and dependent; that acting is the positive and thinking the negative mode of the activity of the self. For the ideas in which thinking terminates are themselves dependent upon and refer to the existents upon which the self operates directly as an Agent.

If we now turn to consider the other aspect of the question, 'What is an *actum*?' we find another contrast, in terms of which we can seek the answer. The opposite of *actio* is *cogitatio*. The opposite of *actum* is *eventum*. An act is contrasted with and distinguished from an event. An action is something that is done, while an event is something that is not done, but happens. Both, in principle, are open to observation, as processes of change. The fact that we distinguish between them involves the assumption that the changes we observe in the world may be either acts or events. The distinction clearly refers to the mode of their occurrence. If the observed changes are acts, then they are made by an agent and have their source in his intention to produce changes in the world. If they are events they do not have their source in the intentionality of an agent. Primarily, it would seem, the conception of an 'event' is negative. It is the idea of a change which cannot be referred to an agent, and which is therefore not an act. Where there is any danger that a particular change might be thought to be an act when it is not we call it an accident. The maid who has broken a valuable dish may excuse herself by saying, 'I didn't break it it just happened. It was an accident'. I would suggest that the idea of an 'event' is in fact derived from the idea of an action through the recognition of such accidents. The primitive tendency of the mind is to refer all changes to agents. Where they cannot be referred to human agency they are referred to some superhuman agent. It is by the inhibition of this tendency to refer all changes to the intentionality of an agent that the concept of 'event' arises. It is the concept of a change which is not intended.

The consideration of accident, that is to say, events which happen in the course of action, apart from the intention of the agent, reveals more than the contrast between *actum* and *eventum*. It also shows that the distinction between them is not contained in them. Both act and event are observable changes in the physical world. As such, they are indistinguishable. By this I mean merely that in principle it is not possible to infer that 'X is an event and not an act' from observation. Such an inference is formally illicit, for the question involved is whether observed matter of fact does or does not express the intentionality of an agent. This can be seen most easily in the case of an accident where a motive for producing the change which happens accidentally is present. The situation is common in trials for murder, where intention has to be proved, and the accused is not allowed to plead guilty, i.e., to admit intention. The facts need not be in dispute. The dead man may have been killed by a bullet fired from a revolver admittedly held by the accused. The defence may be that the accused did not mean to fire, but that the trigger was pulled accidentally. In such cases a presumption of intention can be established in various ways; but however strong it may be it cannot amount to demonstration. The evidence is necessarily circumstantial. My contention is that, in principle, this is true in all cases where intention is concluded from data which are purely matters of observed fact. In other words, there could be no distinction between *actum* and *eventum* for a pure Subject. The distinction can be made only by an Agent, and rests upon his experience of *actio*.

Yet we can and do judge that some observed changes in the physical world involve action; and we do so not merely with varying degrees of probability, but with absolute certainty. We judge with certainty, and merely by inspection, that Westminster Cathedral and the Forth Bridge were intentionally constructed by human action, and could not have happened in the course of Nature. We do not need historical evidence of their building to help us. We know it merely by looking at them. How we know this we need not now enquire. It will be admitted, I imagine, that our certainty is bound up with our direct knowledge of human action. What is important for us is to notice that it implies that we have a knowledge of action which would be impossible if we were merely Subjects for whom the world was merely Object. We shall return to this point later. But before passing to another point, we may note that the reverse is not true. We can never be certain, in the same sense, that any change in the world is a mere event. We can, no doubt, be certain that many events are not acts of human agents. But how can we disprove the contention of a theistic hypothesis that all events, in the last analysis, are acts of God? At the most we could perhaps show that we have no good grounds for supposing this; though in fact I believe that even that is not demonstrable. Our certainty about action is of a higher order than our knowledge of events.

The distinction between acts and events gives rise to the effort to account for events. If an observed change is recognized as *action* it is thereby accounted for, and no further question arises. But if it is recognized as an event, it is not accounted for. The recognition amounts to the negative judgment, 'This change is *not* the deed of an agent'. An alternative source of the change is then required. In modern thought the name for such an alternative source of change is the term 'cause'. The idea of a cause is the idea of a source of change which is not an agent, and does not involve intention.

The recognition of the distinction between *act* and *event* thus has a direct bearing upon the problem of causality. In the first place it shows that the proposition 'Every event has a cause' is perfectly compatible with the proposition, 'No action has a cause'. Indeed, if 'no action is an event' and 'no event is an action', and if the term 'cause' means a source of change which is not *actio*, then the two propositions imply one another. And it follows from this that there is a definite contradiction in talking of the cause of an action. To do so is simply to imply that it is not an action.

Secondly, since in principle it is not possible to distinguish between *actum* and *eventum* by inspection — *actio* not being observable — it is always possible to regard as events all actions in which I myself am not involved as agent. This is merely to say that it is possible to accept the determinist position without being open to logical refutation except in one point — the point at which the assertion of determinism involves me in action. At that point, to assert determinism is to assert that I am not asserting anything. For determinism is the denial of intentionality, and an unintentional assertion is nonsense.

Thirdly, it explains the tendency in science to give up the notion of causality altogether and substitute the notion of law. As Professor Collingwood has recently argued, in a paper read before the Aristotelian Society, there is no ground at all for maintaining that every event has a cause, and the idea of causation which rests upon this so-called axiom will not bear examination. The reason for this, I suggest, is that the idea of an event having a cause is an attempt to think an event on the analogy of an act, while at the same time denying that it can be referred to an agent. The cause is that which is responsible for the production of the event. It is also something which is not an agent, and therefore cannot be responsible for anything, or produce anything. Thus the cause is at once an agent and not an agent. As a result, whatever we assign as the cause appears itself to be an effect which demands a cause to account for it. This negation of agency is not a pure invention to account for the idea of causality. It is what happens when I accept as an accident what I had at first taken to be a deliberate act. In that case I simply agree that there was no *actio* involved, and that therefore the agent is not responsible for the change under consideration. If I am not satisfied to leave the matter there, I shall proceed to ask, in effect, 'If *actio* is not the source of the change, what is?'. I am then committed to the effort to discover something which has the same functional relation to the observed change as *action* would have had if it had been an *actum*, but which is not *actio*. I look for something which functions as if it were an agent, but is not an agent, which behaves in a fashion analogous to acting, but without acting. Yet if we could find anything of the kind, it would clearly *be* an agent, and the change would be his act.

The search for causes, then, depends upon a preoccupation with action, even if it is only half-conscious. But the effort to establish a pure science is an effort to exclude the reference to action and the agent and to describe the world merely as Object for a Subject. This involves the exclusion of all references to action, as well as the suppression of all interest in action. The search for causes must therefore disappear, since that involves both a reference to and an interest in action. All changes then appear as events, even if in fact they are *acta*, and are accepted as such. The task involved is only the classification and description of changes, not the discovery of what is responsible for their happening. What then comes into prominence is the recurrence of events, and in particular the recurrence of sequences of events. The task is the determination, description and correlation of these recurrent sequences, and its goal is the statement of a law, that is to say, the description of an observed pattern of change which recurs (without modification or with a calculable modification) in a continuous process. If the analogue of the idea of causality in personal activity is action, the analogue of the idea of law is habit. I believe that the idea of laws of behaviour in Nature is derived from the idea of habit just as definitely as the idea of causality is derived from the notion of action. But the attempt to demonstrate this lies beyond the proper scope of the present paper.

My intention has been limited to the effort to formulate the question 'What is action?' in a way which will indicate some of its implications. The conclusion which I offer for further consideration is that modern philosophy is incapable of answering the question. The reason for this is that all modern philosophy is an analysis of reflective experience. It defines the Self as Subject and remains within the Subject–Object relation. And action cannot be Object for a Subject. As Subject the Self stands over against the Object, and does not act upon it. Therefore the Object can never be *actum*, and no activity of the Subject, *qua* subject, can ever be *actio*. That the Self is Subject is not in question. What must be denied is that the Self can be *defined* as a Subject. The Self can never be merely Subject, for this would mean that it was pure receptivity, and inherently inactive. Indeed the Self as a Subject is the Self as a non-agent; this merely formulates the fact that we can refrain from acting and reflect. But in the last analysis, this negation of action is itself an action — the deliberative limitation of action to subjective ends. The Self can be Subject only because it is Agent and its Subjecthood is dependent upon its own Agency. Or again, the Subject is the knower, not the thinker. Where I know, I do not think. I think when I do not know, in order to achieve knowledge. The thinker is therefore the agent whose *actio* is reflected back upon himself and so limited to producing changes in his own ideas. He is the agent whose actions are not in the world, because they produce no changes in the world, but only in ideas about the world. If, then, philosophy accepts the Subject–Object relation as defining the relation of the Self to the world, and takes its analysis seriously, it must deny thinking. It reaches the conclusion 'I do *not* think'. This may mean either 'I know', and so be equivalent to the denial or error; or it may mean '*I* do not think'; in other words 'the thinking is not mine'. In this case either there is an Absolute thinker who does the thinking, and I am the knower or Subject who intuits the process; or else there *is* no thinking, and what we call 'thinking' is the process of the world (and not the process of ideas) which I merely observe. But if the Absolute is thinker he cannot also be Subject, since this merely reproduces the problem the Absolute was dragged in to solve; or else there is neither thinking nor action at all. Nor is there, of course, either truth or error, or any need for an Absolute, since there is no problem for which he could be the solution.

This is the dilemma of our philosophy. If we do not think, then we do not think either rightly or wrongly, and there is no problem to solve. If we do think, then we know that we are agents; for to assert that I think is to assert that I am capable of '*actio*' which has knowledge as its end.

Yet this *actio* has as its *actum* the production of a change which can only be defined negatively, as a change which makes no difference in the external world, which is not open to observation, which is not an element in the process of Nature. This implies a knowledge of action which *does* produce changes in the real world; but it also implies that such knowledge is not given in the course of reflection. For in reflection the Agent refrains from changing the Object, in order to know it as it is. He becomes a Subject, standing over against the Object. And if he makes himself Object in reflection, then he appears to himself as something that he contemplates, and his activity as a process of events. *Actio* in other words is not open to observation, even in introspection. For the Subject, all changes appear merely to happen. Yet we know that there is action and that it is distinguishable from mere happening. We know that actions are not processes. If we did not, we could not know that there was thinking. For thought is not a mental process. To describe it as a process is to imply that it is *not* thought. It is to describe it as mere Object for a Subject, as not *actum* but *eventum*. A thought is the act of an Agent in reflection; and therefore refers beyond itself to the world in which he *exists* in action.

Three

Reason in the Emotional Life

What is emotional reason? The question, I imagine, seems a strange one, and that itself is highly significant. Our lives belong to a stage in human development in which reason has been dissociated from the emotional life and is contrasted with it. Reason means to us thinking and planning, scheming and calculating. It carries our thoughts to science and philosophy, to the counting-house or the battlefield, but not to music and laughter and love. It does not make us think of religion or loyalty or beauty, but rather of that state of tension which knits our brows when we apply our minds to some knotty problem or devise schemes to cope with a difficult situation. We associate reason with a state of mind which is cold, detached and unemotional. When our emotions are stirred we feel that reason is left behind and we enter another world — more colourful, more full of warmth and delight, but also more dangerous. If we become egocentric, if we forget that we are parts of one small part of the development of human life, we shall be apt to imagine that this has always been so and always must be so; that reason is just thinking; that emotion is just feeling; and that these two aspects of our life are in the eternal nature of things distinct and opposite; very apt to come into conflict and requiring to be kept sternly apart. We shall even be in danger of slipping back into a way of thinking from which we had begun to emerge; of thinking that emotion belongs to the animal nature in us, and reason to the divine; that our emotions are unruly and

[1] From 'Reason in the Emotional Life I', *Reason and Emotion* (London: Faber, 1935), pp. 3–15.

fleshly, the source of evil and disaster, while reason belongs to the
divine essence of the thinking mind which raises us above the
level of the brutes into communion with the eternal.

Yet, though this seems to be true, it can hardly be the whole
truth about the stage of human development to which we belong.
For after all, here we are discussing the question. Somehow or
other a doubt has arisen, and we have begun to wonder whether
we are right in dissociating the two aspects of our experience. We
are asking now: 'Is this attitude right? *Is* reason a matter of intellect and logical thought? Is it really separated from the emotional
life that surges beneath it in the depths? Or is there reason in the
emotional life itself?' Thought has begun to doubt its own monop-
oly of reason. As soon as that doubt enters the very basis of our
civilization begins to shake, and there arises, first dimly in the
depths of us, but soon penetrating more and more clearly into
consciousness, the cry for a new heaven and a new earth. The
doubt and the question mark the opening of a new phase in
human development.

We must keep that large prospect before the eyes of our imagination, when we begin to think about the emotional life. We must
not think of it only in relation to our own emotional stresses. All of
us, if we are really alive, are disturbed now in our emotions. We
are faced by emotional problems that we do not know how to
solve. They distract our minds, fill us with misgiving, and sometimes threaten to wreck our lives. That is the kind of experience to
which we are all committed. If anyone thinks they are peculiar to
the difficulties of his own situation, let him overcome his shyness
and talk a little about them to other people. He will discover that
he is not a solitary unfortunate. We shall make no headway with
these questions unless we begin to see them, and keep on seeing
them, not as our private difficulties but as the growing pains of a
new world of human experience. Our individual tensions are
simply the new thing growing through us into the life of mankind. When we can see them steadily in this universal setting,
then and then only will our private difficulties become really significant.

If we are to discover the nature of emotional reason we must
first be sure about what we mean by reason in general. It is, in the
first place, that which distinguishes us from the world of organic

life; which makes us men and women — super-organic. It is the characteristic of personal life. This, however, is only a formal statement. We want to know what are the particular ways in which reason reveals itself in human behaviour. One of the most obvious is the power of speech. Another is the capacity to invent and use tools. Another is the power to organize social life. Behind all these there lies the capacity to make a choice of purposes and to discover and apply the means of realizing our chosen ends. We might go on to draw up a list of such peculiarly personal activities; though it would probably not reveal immediately the root from which they all spring. There are, however, certain persistent cultural expressions of human life which are in a special sense characteristic of our rational nature at its best. These are science, art, and religion. This calls attention to one point at least which is highly significant. Whatever is a characteristic and essential expression of human nature must be an expression of reason. We must recognize, then, that if we wish to discover what reason is we must examine religion and art just as much as science. A conception of reason which is applicable to science but not to religion or art must be a false conception, or at least an inadequate one. Now the obvious difference between science on the one hand and art and religion on the other it that science is intellectual while art and religion are peculiarly bound up with the emotional side of human life. They are not primarily intellectual. This at once forces us to conclude that there must be an emotional expression of reason as well as an intellectual one. Thinking is obviously not the only capacity which is characteristically human and personal.

The definition of reason which seems to me most satisfactory is this. Reason is the capacity to behave in terms of the nature of what is not ourselves. We can express this briefly by saying that reason is the capacity to behave in terms of the nature of the object, that is to say, to behave objectively. Reason is thus our capacity for objectivity.[2] When we wish to determine why anything behaves as it does, we normally assume that it behaves in terms of its own nature. This means that we need only find out how it is constituted to understand why it responds to a particular stimulus in a particular way. We are apt to make the same

---

[2]   A fuller and more technical discussion of this definition can be found in my book, *Interpreting the Universe*, chapter VI.

assumption when we are considering how human beings behave. When we do this we are met by a special difficulty which is usually discussed as the difficulty about the freedom of the will. The controversy about free will is insoluble, not because the facts referred to are irreconcilable, but because the problem itself is wrongly conceived. We are looking for something in the inner constitution of the human being to explain the peculiar nature of his behaviour. We are still assuming that he must necessarily behave in terms of his own nature, like anything else. It is precisely this assumption that is at fault. Reason is the capacity to behave, not in terms of our own nature, but in terms of our knowledge of the nature of the world outside. Let me give you a simple example. A little boy starts to run across a busy street. His mother sees him from the pavement and sees that he is in imminent danger of running in front of a motor car. Her natural impulse is to call out to him in terror. If she did so she would be acting subjectively in terms of her own natural constitution, responding to a stimulus from the environment. But she does not. She recognizes that to shout to the boy would only increase his danger by distracting his attention, so she suppresses her impulse. Her behaviour is rational, because it is determined not by her subjective impulse but by her recognition of the nature of the situation outside her. She acts in terms of the nature of the object.

It is easy to see that science and all the practical applications of science depend upon reason, in the sense in which we have just defined it. Science rests upon the desire to know things in their objective nature. Behind this lies the desire to be able to use what is in the world through a knowledge of its nature, that is to say, the desire to increase our capacity for acting in terms of the nature of the object. The extent to which we can behave in terms of the nature of the world outside us depends, quite obviously, upon the extent of our knowledge of the world outside. Where objective knowledge fails us we can only act subjectively, on impulse. It is thus the effort to create the conditions of rational activity that gives rise to science.

Now, the main difficulty that faces us in the development of a scientific knowledge of the world lies not in the outside world but in our own emotional life. It is the desire to retain beliefs to which we are emotionally attached for some reason or other. It is the tendency to make the wish father to the thought. Science itself, therefore, is emotionally conditioned. If we are to be scientific in our thoughts, then, we must be ready to subordinate our wishes and desires to the nature of the world. So long as we want things to be other than they are we cannot see things as they are or act in terms of their real nature. We colour the world with our own illusions. Reason demands that our beliefs should conform to the nature of the world, not to the nature of our hopes and ideals.

In this field, therefore, the discovery of truth must be from the subjective side a process of disillusionment. The strength of our opposition to the development of reason is measured by the strength of our dislike of being disillusioned. We should all admit, if it were put to us directly, that it is good to get rid of illusions, but in practice the process of disillusionment is painful and disheartening. We all confess to the desire to get at the truth, but in practice the desire for truth is the desire to be disillusioned. The real struggle centres in the emotional field, because reason is the impulse to overcome bias and prejudice in our own favour, and to allow our feelings and desires to be fashioned by things outside us, often by things over which we have no control. The effort to achieve this can rarely be pleasant or flattering to our self-esteem. Our natural tendency is to feel and to believe in the way that satisfies our impulses. We all like to feel that we are the central figure in the picture, and that our fate ought to be different from that of everybody else. We feel that life should make an exception in our favour. The development of reason in us means overcoming all this. Our real nature as persons is to be reasonable and to extend and develop our capacity for reason. It is to acquire greater and greater capacity to act objectively and not in terms of our subjective constitution. That is reason, and it is what distinguishes us from the organic world, and makes us super-organic.

It is precisely the same problem that faces us in the field of morality. Morality, after all, is merely a demand for rational behaviour, and its difficulty is only the difficulty of overcoming our own natural bias in favour of ourselves and those we love, and demanding that life shall show us and them special consideration. Morality demands that we should act 'in light of eternity', that is, in terms of things as they really are and of people as they really are, and not in terms of our subjective inclinations and private sympathies.

Now we can attack the main issue. All life is activity. Mere thinking is not living. Yet thinking, too, is an activity, even if it is an activity which is only real in its reference to activities which are practical. Now, every activity must have an adequate motive, and all motives are emotional. They belong to our feelings, not to our thoughts. At the most our thoughts may restrict and restrain, or direct and guide, our actions. They can determine their form but not their substance. Even this they can only do by rousing emotions which check or alter the primary motives. Thought is always subsidiary to activity even when we are not directly aware of it. The rationality that appears in thought is itself the reflection of a rationality that belongs to the motives of action. It follows that none of our activities, not even the activities of thinking, can express our reason unless the emotions which produce and sustain them are rational emotions.

What can it mean, then, to distinguish between rational and irrational feelings? We are in the habit of saying that our feelings are just felt. They can't be either true or false; they just are what they are. Our thoughts, on the other hand, can be true or false. About that we have no difficulty. Yet, if we think carefully, we shall realize that there is no special difference between feelings and thoughts in this respect. Our thoughts are just what we think. We just think them, and they are what they are. How then can they be either true or false? The answer is that their truth or falsity does not lie in them but in a relation between them and the things to which they refer. True thoughts are thoughts which refer properly to reality, and which are thought in terms of the nature of the object to which they refer. Why should our feelings be in any different case? It is true that they are felt and that they are what they are felt to be, just like our thoughts. But they also refer to things outside us. If I am angry I am angry at something or somebody, though I may not always be able to say precisely what it is. Thought is similar. We are often unable to say precisely what it is that we are thinking about, but it is always something. Since our feelings, then, refer to what is outside them, to some object about which they are felt, why should they not refer rightly or wrongly to their object, just like thoughts? Why should they not be proper feelings when they are in terms of the nature of the object, and improper feelings when they are not in terms of the nature of the object? When we put it in this way, we recognize that this is a distinction which we are always making. To a person who is terribly afraid of a mouse we are quite accustomed to say that there is nothing really to be afraid of. Her fear is not is terms of the real nature of the situation. It is subjective. We can acknowledge, therefore, without any difficulty, that feelings can be rational or irrational in precisely the same way as thoughts, through the correctness or incorrectness of their reference to reality. In thinking thoughts we think the things to which the thoughts refer. In feeling emotions we feel the things to which the emotions refer. And, therefore, we can feel rightly or wrongly. The only one of the great philosophers who recognized this parallelism between thought and feeling, and who maintained that our feelings could be true or false, was Plato. He insisted on it both in the *Republic* and in the *Philebus*. This view of Plato's has usually been treated by commentators as a forgivable eccentricity in Plato's thought, like his attitude to art and artists. It seems to me not merely true but of much more profound significance than Plato himself recognized. It is not that our feelings have a secondary and subordinate capacity for being rational or irrational. It is that reason is primarily an affair of emotion, and that the rationality of thought is the derivative and secondary one. For if reason is the capacity to *act* in terms of the nature of the object, it is emotion which stands directly behind activity determining its substance and direction, while thought is related to action indirectly and through emotion, determining only its form, and that only partially.

The chief difficulty in the development of emotional reason lies in the surprising fact that we know relatively little about our own emotional life. We are apt to know more about other people's. It is a commonplace that in all matters which touch us closely it is very difficult to be sure of our own motives. Rather than admit to motives which would injure our self-esteem we prevent them from entering our consciousness or allow them to appear only in forms which disguise and misrepresent their real nature. Modern psychology has been very much concerned to develop various technical methods of overcoming the forces which repress these motives, and its success has been sufficient at least to reveal to what an extent our emotional life is unconscious. But in fact psycho-analysis has only extended and developed a knowledge which we all possess. We continually recognize in other people motives and feelings of which they themselves are quite ignorant. Let me illustrate this by a story of my own invention. It is about three friends, Jane and Josephine and Peter. They are all young. Jane is wealthy and influential. Josephine is a struggling young artist. Both of them are interested in Peter, and Peter is interested in both of them. Josephine has long cherished a desire to continue her art studies in Rome and has applied for a scholarship which would enable her to go. But she is torn between her desire to go abroad and her growing interest in Peter. Jane uses her influence to get the scholarship for Josephine, and succeeds. She carries the good news to Josephine and in great excitement tells her how hard she had worked to get it for her. She is very astonished and hurt to find that Josephine receives the news very coldly and is not properly grateful. At that Jane feels very angry with Josephine.

Jane confides all this to a friend of hers called Peggy. Peggy suggests that the explanation is a simple one. Josephine is feeling sad at having to leave her friends and has been growing very fond of Peter. Jane admits that Josephine is fond of Peter but feels quite sure that that can't be the reason. Josephine, she says, would never allow anything of that kind to interfere with her art. In any case, it is very good for Peter that she should go. Peter is very sensitive and Josephine's artistic temperament plays havoc with his nerves. Jane has often noticed it. Indeed when she was working to get the scholarship for Josephine, she had Peter's welfare in her mind too. Whether Josephine is grateful or not, she doesn't care. She is proud to have been able to serve both her friends.

What was Jane's real motive? All her friends told themselves — and each other — what it was. But did Jane know? Probably not at all. She would have been very hurt if anyone had presumed to enlighten her. At any rate there is no need for me to explain. The point of the story for our present purpose is this: the reasons we give ourselves for our activities, and even more certainly the reasons we give to other people for them, rarely express our real motive, and never the whole of our motive. When we ask ourselves why we behaved as we did, we often find ourselves insisting to ourselves, with a certain inner stress, upon the reasons that we give. That feeling of insistence is always adequate evidence that the real motive is a different one, and one that is hidden from ourselves. Such hidden motives are necessarily subjective. They are necessarily the expression not of reason but of subjective impulses. They cannot be in terms of our conscious recognition of the true nature of the situation.

It is extremely difficult to become aware of this great hinterland of our minds, and to bring our emotional life, and with it the motives which govern our behaviour, fully into consciousness. This is peculiarly true of contemporary people. It is not nearly so true of primitive men. The nineteenth century in particular was the climax of a long period of social repression in which the intellectual development of reason was the main effort and the emotional life was considered chiefly as an intrusive force which prevented the achievement of that calmness which is necessary for the proper functioning of thought. But that development itself brings us back at last to the emotional life. The development of science finally must direct its attention to personality itself; and as soon as it does this it is directed upon the emotional sources of all personal activity. It is because it is so difficult for us to bring our unconscious motives into consciousness that at last we find ourselves driven to make the attempt. That is why so much of the interest of contemporary life is centred upon emotional experience. It means the beginning of the task of developing emotional reason in man. In this, as in most things, it is the first step that is the most difficult. Jane's emotional development will begin when she realizes that she was jealous of Josephine and wanted to get her out of the way. The probable effect of this realization will be that she will say to herself 'What a horrible little worm I am', and begin to revel in despising herself. Such self-abasement is just as unreasonable, perhaps even more unreasonable, than her previous state of mind. It is as a compensation which still enables her to be concerned with herself. It is still childish, immature and egocentric. Self-pity and self-disgust are just as irrational as self-assertion. The real problem of the development of emotional reason is to shift the centre of feeling from the self to the world outside. We can only begin to grow up into rationality when we begin to see our own emotional life not as the centre of things but as part of the development of humanity.

The field in which emotional reason expresses itself most directly is the field of art. The artist is directly concerned to express his emotional experience of the world. His success depends upon the rationality of his emotions. It is not enough that the artist should express his emotional reaction to the world. If his feelings are merely subjective reactions, his work will be bad. What will make it valuable or significant is the way in which his emotions refer to the world. The artist expresses that nature of the objective world as apprehended in emotion. As a result, our own experience of works of art shows the same distinction between those which affect us subjectively and those which reveal the world to us in its real significance. Some pictures, for instance, we appreciate because they touch off in our minds associations which are pleasant and exciting. They act upon us merely as a stimulus to thoughts and feelings which we enjoy for their own sake. But such pictures are artistically bad. There are others which move us in an entirely different way, because they contain their significance in themselves. They do not set us to enjoy our own feelings. They make us enjoy *themselves*, and they refer us to the significance of the world outside.

These true works of art are more difficult to appreciate. They do something to us, often, if they are contemporary; something that we object to. They involve some disillusionment that we dislike, and they are not immediately exciting. They deny us the opportunity of revelling in our own sensations and force us to be objective. The reason is that objective emotion is not a mere reaction to a stimulus. It is an immediate appreciation of the value and significance of real things. Emotional reason is our capacity to apprehend objective values. This point, important as it is, I have no time to develop at length. I must conclude by drawing your attention to its final expression in our relations with one another. Love, which is the fundamental positive emotion characteristic of human beings, can be either subjective and irrational, or objective and rational. In feeling love for another person, I can either experience a pleasurable emotion which he stimulates in me, or I can love *him*. We have, therefore, to ask ourselves, is it really the other person that I love, or is it myself? Do I enjoy him or do I enjoy myself in being with him? Is he just an instrument for keeping me pleased with myself, or do I feel his existence and his reality to be important in themselves? The difference between these two kinds of love is the ultimate difference between organic and personal life. It is the difference between rational and irrational emotion. The capacity to love objectively is the capacity which makes us persons. It is the ultimate source of our capacity to behave in terms of the object. It is the core of rationality.

Four

Mother and Child

There is a widespread belief, of which Aristotle is probably the original source, that the human infant is an animal organism which becomes rational, and acquires a human personality, in the process of growing up. In Aristotle's terminology, the baby is *potentially* but not *actually* rational. It realizes this potentiality through a process of habit-formation; and in this process a 'character' is formed. 'Character' is an orderly organization of the original animal impulses, so that they no longer function independently as motives of behaviour, but as elements in a system. Thus the mature human being acts for the satisfaction of his character, of himself as a whole in a whole life, and this satisfaction we call 'happiness'. The child, like that animal, acts for the satisfaction of isolated impulses as they arise, and this satisfaction is 'pleasure'. We might then illustrate the characteristic difference between rational and non-rational behaviour by saying that when an animal is hungry it goes in search of food; but when a man is hungry he looks at his watch to see how long it will be before his next meal.

The Aristotelian theory interests us only because of the influence it has had, and still has, upon our customary ways of thinking. If the notion that children are little animals who acquire the characteristics of rational humanity through education, whose personalities are 'formed' by the pressures brought to bear upon them as they grow up — if this notion seems to us simple common sense, and matter of everyday observation — it is because we share the traditional outlook and attitude of a culture which has

---

[1]   From 'Mother and Child', *Persons in Relation* (London: Faber, 1961), pp. 44–63.

been moulded by Greek and in particular by Aristotelian ideas. So much of common sense is the relic of past philosophies!

Whatever its origin, this view is radically false; and our first task is to uncover the error on which it rests and to replace it by a more adequate view. In his important contribution to psycho-therapeutic theory, *The Origin of Love and Hate*, the late Dr Ian Suttie asserted roundly that the human infant is less like an animal that the human adult.[2] This goes too far, perhaps, in the opposite direction, but it is a valuable corrective to the traditional view. The root of the error is the attempt to understand the field of the personal on a biological analogy, and so through organic categories. The Greek mode of thought was naturally biological, or zoomorphic. The Greek tradition has been strongly reinforced by the organic philosophies of the nineteenth century and the consequent development of evolutionary biology. This in turn led to the attempt to create evolutionary sciences in the human field, particularly in its social aspect. The general result of these convergent cultural activities — the Romantic movement, the organic philosophies, idealist or realist, and evolutionary science — was that contemporary thought about human behaviour, individual and social, became saturated with biological metaphors, and moulded itself to the requirements of an organic analogy. It became the common idiom to talk of ourselves as organisms and of our societies as organic structures; to refer to the history of society as an evolutionary process and to account for all human action as an adaptation to environment.

It was assumed, and still is assumed in many quarters, that this way of conceiving of human life is scientific and empirical and therefore the truth about us. It is in fact not empirical; it is *a priori* and analogical. Consequently it is not, in the strict sense, even scientific. For this concept, and the categories of understanding which go with it, were not discovered by a patient unbiased examination of the facts of human activity. They were discovered, at best, through an empirical and scientific study of the facts of plant and animal life. They were applied by analogy to the human field on the *a priori* assumption that human life must exhibit the same structure.

[2]   Suttie, *op. cit.*, p. 15.

The practical consequences are in the end disastrous; but they do reveal the erroneous character of the assumption. To affirm the organic conception in the personal field is implicitly to deny the possibility of action; yet the meaning of the conception lies in its reference to action. We can only act upon the organic conception by transforming it into a determinant of our intention. It becomes an ideal to be achieved. We say, in effect, 'Society is organic; therefore let us make it organic, as it ought to be'. The contradiction here is glaring. If society is organic, then it is meaningless to say that it *ought* to be. For if it ought to be, then it is *not*. The organic conception of the human, as a practical ideal, is what we now call the totalitarian state. It rests on the practical contradiction which corresponds to this theoretical one. 'Man is not free', it runs, 'therefore he ought not to be free'. If organic theory overlooks human freedom, organic practice must suppress it.

It is one of the major intentions which animate this book to help towards the eradication of this fundamental and dangerous error. It may therefore be advisable, at this point, to issue a flat denial, without qualifications. We are not organisms, but persons. The nexus of relations which unites us in a human society is not organic but personal. Human behaviour cannot be understood, but only caricatured, if it is represented as an adaptation to environment; and there is no such process as social evolution but, instead, a history which reveals a precarious development and possibilities both of progress and of retrogression. It is true, as we have argued already, that the personal necessarily includes an organic aspect. But it cannot be defined in terms of its own negative; and this organic aspect is continuously qualified by its inclusion, so that it cannot even be properly abstracted except through a prior understanding of the personal structure in which it is an essential, though subordinate, component. A descent from the personal is possible, in theory and indeed in practice; but there is no way for thought to ascend from the organic to the personal. The organic conception of man excludes, by its very nature, all the characteristics in virtue of which we are human beings. To include them we must change our categories and start afresh from the beginning.

We start then where all human life starts, with infancy; at the stage of human existence where, if at all, we might expect to find a biological conception adequate. If it is not adequate to explain the behaviour of a newborn child, than *a fortiori* it must be completely inadequate as an account of human life in its maturity. The most obvious fact about the human infant is his total helplessness. He has no power of locomotion, nor even of co-ordinated movement. The random movements of limbs and trunk and head of which he is capable do not even suggest an unconscious purposiveness. The essential physiological rhythms are established, and perhaps a few automatic reflexes. Apart from these, he has no power of behaviour; he cannot respond to any external stimulus by a reaction which would help to defend him from danger or to maintain his own existence. In this total helplessness, and equally in the prolonged period of time which must elapse before he can fend for himself at all, the baby differs from the young of all animals. Even the birds are not helpless in this sense. The chicks of those species which nest at a distance from their food supply must be fed by their parents till they are able to fly. But they peck their way out of the egg, and a lapwing chick engaged in breaking out of the shell will respond to its mother's danger call by stopping its activity and remaining quite still.

We may best express this negative difference, with reference to biological conceptions, by saying that the infant has no instincts. That human beings have no instincts is, I understand, a conclusion at which many psychologists have arrived, and to which psychology as a whole increasingly tends. That this has been a slow process arises from the vagueness of the term instinct. If we insist on defining it in terms of strict biological usage, the conclusion follows at once. An eminent biologist to whom I once referred the question even doubted whether there were any unambiguous instances of instinctive behaviour among the higher animals. For our purpose we may define the term instinct as a specific adaptation to environment which does not require to be learned. The term 'specific' here means 'sufficiently definite to fulfil its biological function'. A 'specific' adaptation is a response to an external stimulus which is biologically adequate, which does not require to be completed, though it may be improved, by any process of learning. If this is what we mean by 'instinct' then it is clear that we are born with none. All purposive human behaviour has to be learned. To begin with, our responses to stimulus are, without exception, biologically random.

There must, however, be a positive side to this. The baby must be fitted by nature at birth to the conditions into which he is born; for otherwise he could not survive. He is, in fact, 'adapted', to speak paradoxically, to being unadapted, 'adapted' to a complete dependence upon an adult human being. He is made to be cared for. He is born into a love-relationship which is inherently personal. Not merely his personal development, but his very survival depends upon the maintaining of this relation; he depends for his existence, that is to say, upon intelligent understanding, upon rational foresight. He cannot think for himself, yet he cannot do without thinking; so someone else must think for him. He cannot foresee his own needs and provide for them; so he must be provided for by another's foresight. He cannot do himself what is necessary to his own survival and development. It must be done for him by another who can, or he will die.

The baby's 'adaptation' to his 'environment' consists in his capacity to express his feelings of comfort or discomfort; of satisfaction and dissatisfaction with his condition. Discomfort he expresses by crying; comfort by gurgling and chuckling, and very soon by smiling and crowing. The infant's cry is a call for help to the mother, an intimation that he needs to be cared for. It is the mother's business to interpret his cry, to discover by taking thought whether he is hungry, or cold, or being pricked by a pin, or ill; and having decided what is the matter with him, to do for him what he needs. If she cannot discover what is the matter, she will consult someone else, or send for the doctor. His expression of satisfaction is closely associated with being cared for, with being nursed, with the physical presence of the mother, and particularly with physical contact. It would seem to be, from a biological point of view, unnecessary. There is no obvious utilitarian purpose in it; for the cessation of his cries would be enough to tell the mother that her efforts had succeeded in removing his distress. It seems impossible to account for it except as an expression of satisfaction in the relation itself; in being touched caressingly, attended to and cared for by the mother. This is evidence that the infant has a need which is not simply biological but personal, a need to be in touch with the mother, and in conscious perceptual relation with her. And it is astonishing at what an early age a baby cries not because of any physiological distress, but because he has noticed that he is alone, and is upset by his mother's absence. Then the mere appearance of the mother, or the sound of her voice, is enough to remove the distress and turn his cries into smiles of satisfaction.

Now if we attend to these everyday facts without any theoretical prejudice, it is obvious that the relation of mother and child is quite inadequately expressed in biological terms, and that the attempt to give an organic account of it must lead to a caricature. For to talk of the infant's behaviour as an adaptation to environment ought to mean that he responds to external stimuli in a way that is biologically effective. Yet it is precisely his inability to do this that is the governing factor. Further, when we speak of 'environment' in a biological context, we mean nature, as the source of stimuli and of material for the supply of the organism's needs as well as of dangers to its survival. But the human infant is not in direct relation to nature. His environment is a home, which is not a natural habitat, but a human creation, an institution providing in advance for human needs, biological and personal, through human foresight and artifice. In general, to represent the process of human development, even at his earliest stage, as an organic process, is to represent it in terms which are equally applicable to the development of animals, and therefore to exclude reference to any form of behaviour which is exclusively human; to exclude reference to rationality in any of its expressions, practical or theoretical; reference to action or to knowledge, to deliberate purpose or reflective thought. If this were correct, no infant could ever survive. For its existence and its development depend from the beginning on rational activities, upon thought and action. The baby cannot yet think or act. Consequently he must depend for his life upon the thought and action of others. The conclusion is not that the infant is still an animal which will become rational through some curious organic process of development. It is that he cannot, even theoretically, live an isolated existence; that he is not an independent individual. He lives a common life as one term in a personal relation. Only in the process of development does he learn to achieve a relative independence, and that only by appropriating the techniques of a rational social tradition. All the infant's activities in maintaining his existence are shared and co-operative. He cannot even feed; he has to be fed. The sucking reflex is his sole contribution to his own nutrition, the rest is the mother's.

If we insist on interpreting the facts through biological categories, we shall be committed to talking puerilities about maternal instinct. There is no such thing, of course; if there were, it would have to include some very curious instinctive components, such as a shopping instinct and a dressmaking instinct. Even the term 'mother' in this connection is not a biological term. It means simply the adult who cares for the baby. Usually it will be the woman who bore him, but this is not necessarily so. A human infant does not necessarily die, like an animal, if his mother dies in childbirth. The mother may be an aunt, or an elder sister or a hired nurse. She need not even be a female. A man can do all the mothering that is necessary, if he is provided with a feeding-bottle, and learns how to do it in precisely the same fashion that a woman must learn.

From all this it follows that the baby is not an animal organism, but a person, or in traditional terms, a rational being. The reason is that his life, and even his bodily survival, depends upon intentional activity, and therefore upon knowledge. If nobody intends his survival and acts with intention to secure it, he cannot survive. That he cannot act intentionally, that he cannot even think for himself and has no knowledge by which to live is true, and is of the first importance. It does not signify, however, that he is merely an animal organism; if it did it would mean that he could live by the satisfaction of organic impulse, by reaction to stimulus, by instinctive adaptation to his natural environment. But this is totally untrue. He cannot live at all by any initiative, whether personal or organic, of his own. He can live only through other people and in dynamic relation with them. In virtue of this fact he is a person, for the personal is constituted by the relation of persons. His rationality is already present, though only germinally, in the fact that he lives and can only live by communication. His essential natural endowment is the impulse to communicate with another human being. Perhaps his cry of distress when he wakens alone in the night in his cot in the nursery has no meaning for *him*, but for the mother it has; and as she hurries to him she will respond to it by calling, 'It's all right, darling, mother's coming'.

We can now realize why it is that the activities of an infant, taken as a whole, have a personal and not an organic form. They are not merely motivated, but their motivation is governed by intention. The intention is the mother's, necessarily; the motives, just as necessarily, are the baby's own. The infant is active; if his activities were unmotivated, he would be without any consciousness, and could not even develop a capacity to see or hear. But if he is hungry, he does not begin to feed or go in search of food. His feeding occurs at regular intervals, as part of a planned routine, just as an adult's does. The satisfaction of his motives is governed by the mother's intention. It is part of the routine of family life. Now it is important for us to gain some reliable idea of the structure of personal motivation — in distinction from intention; and since motive and intention operate, in the case of the infant, in different persons, and the baby has no intention of his own, we can do this most easily by studying the original motivational endowment of persons in infancy, before going on to consider the processes of its development. We must ask ourselves, therefore, at this point, what the structure of personal motivation is, as it manifests itself in babyhood.

We can dismiss at once any notion that we are born with a set of 'animal' impulses which later take on a rational form. There is no empirical evidence for anything like this, and it is inherently improbable. In the absence of intention and knowledge, consciousness is motive, as we have seen. This means primarily that a feeling is present which selects the movement which responds to a stimulus. In the absence of any behaviour on the part of an organism, that is, of any activity which is so directed that we can understand it as an adaptation to the environment, we have no ground even for suspecting the existence of a motive, or indeed of consciousness at all. A motive is an element in, or aspect of, a behavioural activity. A specific motive means a specific form of behaviour. To say that any living creature is endowed with a set of motives can only mean that it behaves in a set of distinguishable ways, and that its behaviour is of a kind which requires us to postulate a conscious component.

Now so far as concerns behaviour which is adapted to a natural environment, the human infant does not behave at all. Its movements are conspicuously random. If this were all, we should have no grounds for suspecting the presence of motives, or indeed of consciousness. The baby's movements could quite well be described as automatisms. What prevents this conclusion is an observable progress, with no conspicuous breaks, in the direction of controlled activity. The movements gradually lose their random character and acquire direction and form. But the character of this development is quite unlike that observable even in the highest animals. It does not rapidly produce a capacity to adapt itself to the environment. In the early stages at least, it does not seem to tend in this direction at all. It is quite a long time before the baby learns to walk or to stand or even to crawl; and his early locomotion, so far from making him more capable of looking after himself, increases the dangers of his existence, and the need for constant parental care and watchfulness. Nature leaves the provision for his physiological needs and his well-being to the mother for many years, until indeed he has learned to form his own intentions, and acquired the skill to execute them and the knowledge and foresight which will enable him to act responsibly as a member of a personal community.

The child's progress appears rather to consist in the acquirement of skills, as it were for their own sake, without any distinguishable objective to which they are a means; and the primary stage seems to be concerned with the use of the organs of sense. The baby learns first to discriminate colours and shapes, and to distinguish familiar from unfamiliar complexes of these. Similarly he acquires the skill to distinguish sounds and concatenations of sounds, and to make different sounds at will. Then he learns to correlate sight and touch, acquiring the skill to put his hand on what he sees. In this stage he is learning to discriminate in awareness; acquiring the basic skills which are essential for an awareness of objects, that is, for sense-perception. Because sense-perception is learned so early in life we are very apt to forget that it has to be learned at all; so that we talk of it as though the power to perceive a world of objects were born in us, and that its 'immediacy' is an original datum of human experience. This is not so. Perceiving by means of the senses is an acquired skill, and varies from one person to the next, partly no doubt because of inherited physiological differences; but partly, and probably in most cases to a much larger extent, because some of us carry the process of learning to use our senses farther than others.

We need not attempt to follow this progress in detail. Only a few general observations are necessary for our purpose. We must first notice the hierarchical and systematic character of the process. The child must first learn the simplest elementary skills, whether of sensory discrimination or of movement. His attention, and therefore his consciousness, is concentrated, at any stage, upon acquiring the particular skill he is learning. The learning process is a conscious process. But when a particular lesson has been learned, the child's attention passes beyond it to the acquirement of a wider skill, in which the skill already learned is a component. What he has already learnt to do can now be done without attention, automatically; while attention is directed to learning a new skill for which the first provides an unconscious basis. He must learn to stand before he can learn to walk; to discriminate sounds and to produce articulate sounds before he can learn to speak. Each lower-level skill becomes thus the automatic basis of a higher-level skill to be acquired. In this way a hierarchical system of skills is developed, the lower levels of which support the higher skills automatically as unconscious components.

This process is usually — and rightly — described as the formation of habits, and the integrated system of skills is a system of habits. In an earlier discussion we recognized habit as the negative aspect of an action; as that in action which is not intended because not attended to. It is included in, and governed by intention, but in itself it has an organic character. It is reaction to stimulus. Bearing this in mind, we see that in human behaviour habit takes the place of instinct in animals. It functions in human activity as an instinct does in animal activity. The essential difference is that a habit is consciously acquired. It is a learned response to stimulus, while an instinct is a response to stimulus which does not have to be learned. But this difference carries an important corollary. What has been learned can, in principle, be unlearned and relearned. If this is not in fact the case, particularly with the basic habits which are acquired very early, it is because the changing of habit is a deliberate and conscious process, which requires a sufficient motive to sustain it; and also because to unlearn a basic habit involves a cessation of all those higher-level activities in

which it is an automatic component. It is this functional correspondence of personal habit and animal instinct which lies at the
root of the widespread tendency to describe certain kinds of
human behaviour as instinctive. It would, however, be less misleading to reverse the tendency and to speak of animal instincts as
innate habits.

We may notice next that this aspect of the child's development
has the character of play. Play is activity carried on for its own
sake. It is not, however, random but directed activity. It has a goal;
but the goal is for the sake of the activity. Play is therefore essentially concerned with skill — with its acquirement, its improvement, and its manifestation. The goal is not *substantially* intended;
it functions rather as a test or verification of the skill. We contrast
it with work, which is activity in which skill is not merely dis-
played but used; in which the interest centres in the goal to be
achieved, while the skilled expenditure of energy is merely a
means to the end, for the sake of this end and therefore normally
automatic and unconscious. But the play of children and young
animals, though it is, in this fashion, activity for its own sake, is
not therefore functionless. When seen in relation to the life of the
individual as a whole, it is clearly an exercise or a practising of
skills which are necessary as means to the mature activities of
later life. The young imitate in play the necessary activities of
maturity; so that their play is a way of learning the life of a personal maturity; the animal a life of biological maturity. The difference is a difference in form, not merely in degree of complexity.
We need call attention only to a few of the differences. Firstly, animals in play are, in general, practising and so perfecting skills
which are in some sense already present from the beginning. The
child has to start from scratch, and has to learn everything. All his
skills are acquired. Secondly, the child's acquiring of skills is a
cumulative process. Simple skills are used in acquiring more complex skills, and the process goes on indefinitely. For in learning
them he learns how to learn. Thirdly, at an early stage of the process we begin to suspect the presence of deliberate intention, and
soon we are sure of it. The form of the child's behaviour convinces
us that he knows what he is doing. Opinions will differ as to the
point at which a mere reaction to stimulus gives place to deliberate action; at which the child can form an intention and so foresee

the end which is his goal, and select a means of attaining it. We can be sure, however, that it does not come as a sudden miraculous intrusion; and that it has been present for some time before we can verify its presence as observers. Indeed it would be methodologically correct, even if not empirically necessary, to assume its presence from the beginning, or at least of some capacity of which it is a manifestation, and which expresses itself in overt behaviour as soon as the conditions permit.

This leads us to consider the last of the differences from animal learning to which we must refer. Intention involves knowledge, and knowledge depends upon the acquirement of reflective skills. The basic reflective skill, on which the others depend, is imagination; the formation, definition and coordination of images, especially visual and auditory images. Hand in hand with this there goes the discrimination of feelings, particularly those which are associated with tactual experience; and the coordination of these with sensory images. This development of imagination is primarily, no doubt, a negative aspect of the practical skills we have already considered. But there is also a play of the imagination in which the reflective skills are acquired and exercised for their own sake. We call this phantasy. An important part of the child's play activity is therefore the development of a life of phantasy for its own sake, which is not governed by logic — that is to say, by a practical reference to the Other — but by feeling. There is no good reason to suppose that any but the lowest stage of this acquirement of reflective skills is present in any of the animals.

Finally, we must return to our starting point, from which this discussion of the child's development took its rise. We set out to discover the general principles of an original motivation for human behaviour. Instead, we have talked about the development of habits, laying stress upon the contrast with animal development. For this there were two reasons. The first was that the infant's helplessness, and the random character of its earliest movements, seem hardly to require the presence of a motive consciousness to account for them. But when we consider the development which has its origin in these random movements, particularly the continuity and hierarchical character of their gradual determination as a system of habit, we are forced to conclude that a motivating consciousness is present from the beginning. Automatic reflexes do not develop. They remain with us throughout life in their original form. At most we acquire in some cases a precarious ability to suppress them by deliberative effort. The random character of the movements at the start, if it is the beginning of a process of definition and discrimination, must be motivated by a consciousness which is itself as indefinite as awareness can be. Our earlier analysis of consciousness[3] enables us to give a meaning to this. The infant's original consciousness, even as regards its sensory elements, must be feeling, and feeling at its most primitive and undiscriminated level. What it cannot be is a set of discriminated 'animal impulses', each with its implicit reference to a mode of behaviour, in relation to the environment, which would satisfy them. We have no ground for thinking that the newborn child can distinguish between a feeling of pain, a feeling of sickness and a feeling of hunger. This discrimination, too, we must assume, has to be learned. The most we have a right to assert, on the empirical evidence, is an original capacity to distinguish, in feeling, between comfort and discomfort. We postulate, therefore, an original feeling consciousness, with a discrimination between positive and negative phases.

The second reason for introducing this excursus on the development of skills is that it has only a negative importance for our main subject. It is essential that it should be considered, if only to show that it is not being overlooked. It is important to bear it in mind throughout, if we are not to fall into the error of giving a 'subjective' account of the personal, and so implying the dualism which we have found good reason to reject. But the acquiring of skills, the formation of a system of habits, is only the negative aspect of personal development. Skill is always for the sake of an end beyond it to which it is a means; and even where fully intentional action is required for the formation of a habit, once formed it becomes automatic; attention passes beyond it and it functions as a reaction to stimulus which supports action and is included within action. The progress in skilled behaviour which we have discussed is, then, only the negative aspect of the child's personal development. Habit, we discovered earlier, as the negative aspect of action, has an organic structure; it is reaction to stimulus. We

[3]   *The Self as Agent*, pp. 119 ff.

have therefore been considering the organic aspect of the child's development. For this reason the enthusiast for biological explanation will be tempted to refer to animal analogies at every point and to retort that the differences are merely in complexity, and are open, in principle, to organic formulation. This may be admitted. In the same way, physiological processes are open, in principle, to chemical formulation, through a proper selection of their negative aspect; and the movements of the planets can, in principle, be accounted for on the Ptolemaic hypothesis, though the complexity of the account, and the amount of imaginative ingenuity it would involve, would render it suspect even if it were given.

We selected this negative aspect of the infant's life by the simple device of thinking of him as an isolate, and seeking the origin of his behaviour wholly within himself; by treating him as a self-contained individual. In particular, we referred the form of his behaviour wholly to him. But we have already noted that this is not correct. The form of his behaviour is governed by the intention of the mother, in terms of a personal mode of corporate life into which it must be fitted. Because of this even the negative aspect of the child's development has a rational form, although the intention which rationalizes it has to be, for a considerable time, wholly the mother's. The consequence is that the skills a child acquires, and the form in which he acquires them, fit him to take his place as a member of a personal community, and not to fend for himself in natural surroundings.

The whole of this aspect of human development, then, falls within and helps to constitute its positive aspect. It falls, that is, within the 'You and I' of the mother–child relation. For the mother plays with the child, and the child responds; the child calls for the participation, or at least the attention of the adult, and for the admiration and approval of his success. His play has another character which we omitted to mention. It is not merely an *exercise*, but a *display* of skill. The reference to the mother is pervasive in all the child's activities. He does not merely learn, as animals do, by instinct helped out by trial and error; he is *taught*. *His* acquirement of skills is an education. It is a cooperative process which requires from the start the foresight, judgment and action of a mature person to give it an intentional form. Because of this, the child's development has a continuous reference to the distinction between 'right' and 'wrong'. He learns to await the right time for the satisfaction of his desires; that some activities are permitted and other suppressed; that some things may be played with and others not. He learns, in general, to submit his impulses to an order imposed by another will than his; and to subordinate his own desires to those of another person. He learns, in a word, to submit to reason.

Now the original capacity to feel comfort and discomfort, which we admitted, is a psychological abstraction. It exists only as the motive consciousness of a pattern of behaviour — an original 'adaptation' to the conditions of life. But the total helplessness of the infant makes any directed movement in relation to the environment out of the question. His feeling of comfort or discomfort is, indeed, the motive of an activity of expression, the function of which is to communicate his feeling to the mother, and to elicit a response from her. When he feels uncomfortable he cries; and his cry is an unconscious call for assistance. The mother understands it so, and responds to it by comforting him.

It has commonly been asserted that what distinguishes us from the animals is the gift of speech. There is an obvious truth in this, but it has two defects if used for purposes of definition. The power of speech is sometimes defined as the capacity to express ourselves. This misses an essential point; for the power of speech is as much the capacity to understand what is said to us as it is to say things to other people. The ability to speak is then, in the proper sense, the capacity to enter into reciprocal communication with others. It is our ability to share our experience with one another and so to constitute and participate in a common experience. Secondly, speech is a particular skill; and like all skills it presupposes an end to which it is a means. No one considers that deaf-mutes lack the characteristic which distinguishes them as human beings from the animals. They are merely obliged to discover other means of communication than speech. Long before the child learns to speak he is able to communicate, meaningfully and intentionally, with his mother. In learning language, he is acquiring a more effective and more elaborate means of doing something which he already can do in a crude and more primitive fashion. If this were not so, not merely the child's acquiring speech, but the very existence of language would be an inexplicable mystery. Nor should we forget that he learns to speak by being spoken to; he is taught to speak, and he understands what is said to him before he is able to respond in articulate words.

It would, of course, be possible to find, in animal life, instances in plenty which seem to be, and perhaps actually are, cases of communication. To take these as objections to what has been urged here would be to miss the point. For these are not definitive. In the human infant — and this is the heart of the matter — the impulse to communication is his sole adaptation to the world into which he is born. Implicit and unconscious it may be, yet it is sufficient to constitute the mother–child relation as the basic form of human existence, as a personal mutuality, as a 'You and I' with a common life. For this reason the infant is born a person and not an animal. All his subsequent experience, all the habits he forms and the skills he acquires fall within this framework, and are fitted to it. Thus human experience is, in principle, shared experience; human life, even in its most individual elements, is a common life; and human behaviour carries always, in its inherent structure, a reference to the personal Other. All this may be summed up by saying that the unit of personal existence is not the individual, but two persons in personal relation; and that we are persons not by individual right, but in virtue of our relation to one another. The personal is constituted by personal relatedness. The unit of the personal is not the 'I', but the 'You and I'.

We can now define the original motivation-pattern of personal behaviour. We have recognized, as the minimum of our original motive consciousness, the capacity to feel comfort and discomfort. But the behaviour which is motivated by this distinction is, we now see, an activity which communicates the experience to the mother. The motivation of the infant's behaviour is still bipolar; it has a positive and a negative phase; the negative phase being genetically prior, since it expresses a need for the mother's aid, while the positive expresses satisfaction in the supply of its needs. But both the negative and positive poles have an original and implicit reference to the other person, with whom the infant shares a common life. This original reference to the other is of a definitive importance. It is the germ of rationality. For the character that distinguishes rational from non-rational experience, in all the expressions of reason, is its reference to the Other-than-myself. What we call 'objectivity' is one expression of this — the conscious reference of an idea to an object. But it is to be noted that this is not the primary expression of reason. What is primary, even in respect of reflective thought — is the reference to the other *person*. A true judgment is one which is made by one individual — as every judgment must be — but is valid for all others. Objective thought presupposes this by the assumption that there is a *common* object about which a communication may be made.

The human infant, then, being born into, and adapted to, a common life with the mother, is a person from birth. His survival depends upon reason, that is to say, upon action and not upon reaction to stimulus. We must, therefore, complete our analysis by defining it in its positive personal mode, which contains and is constituted by its negative or organic aspect. The animal has certain needs — for food, for warmth, for protection. It is endowed by nature with specific patterns of behaviour for their satisfaction. The child has the same needs; but it is not so provided. Instead, it has a single need which contains them all — the need for a mother, the need to be cared for. If this need is satisfied then organic needs are provided for. The baby does not feed himself, he is fed. He does not protect himself, he is protected. The provision for his various needs falls within the mother's care as aspects and manifestations of it. They differentiate her caring and give it actuality and systematic form. The baby need do nothing about his organic needs, and therefore need not even be aware of them discriminatingly. Now the positive motive of the mother's caring is her love for the child; it contains, however, and subordinates a negative component of fear — anxiety for the child's welfare. This negative component is essential, since it provides the motive for thought and foresight on the child's behalf, and for provision in advance against the dangers to its life, health and welfare, both in the present and the future. Without it love would be inoperative and ineffectual, a mere sentimentality and therefore unreal.

Now since the mother–child relation is the original unit of personal existence, the motivation of the child's behaviour must be reciprocal, even if this reciprocity is, to begin with, merely implicit. The positive and negative poles of the infant's motivation are the germinal forms of love and fear respectively. The sense of discomfort expressed in the call for the mother is implic-

itly the fear of isolation; and since isolation from the relationship
which constitutes his existence, if it lasts too long, means death, it
is implicitly the fear of death. The sense of comfort communicated
by his expression of delight in being cared for is the germinal form
of love. This bipolar, reciprocal, love and fear motivation is concerned with maintaining the personal relationship in a common
life between mother and child. We need draw attention only to
two characteristics which have a special importance for our further study. The first is that the negative pole, in the child's behaviour as in the mother's, falls within and is subordinated to the
positive. Isolation from the mother, if it becomes permanent, does
involve death. The baby who loses the mother loses his life. But
the fear of isolation functions in the child's life as a means of
bringing the mother's care into active operation and so eliminating the ground for fear. It diversifies the child's experience of the
relationship, and institutes the rhythm of withdrawal and return
to which I referred in the first volume.[4] The second characteristic
is this. There is from the beginning an element of symbolic activity
involved which has no organic or utilitarian purpose, and which
makes the relationship, as it were, an end in itself. The relationship is enjoyed, both by mother and child, for its own sake. The
mother not only does what is needful for the child: she fondles
him, caresses him, rocks him in her arms, and croons to him; and
the baby responds with expression of delight in his mother's care
which have no biological significance. These gestures symbolize a
mutual delight in the relation which unites them in a common life:
they are expressions of affection through which each communicates to the other their delight in the relationship, and they represent, for its own sake, a consciousness of communicating. It is not
long before the baby's cries convey, not some organic distress, but
simply the need for the mother's presence to banish the sense of
loneliness, and to reassure him of her care for him. As soon as she
appears, as soon as the baby is in touch with her again, the crying
ceases, and is replaced by a smile of welcome.

---

[4]   *The Self as Agent*, p. 181.

Five

The Rhythm of Withdrawal and Return

The differentiation of the original personal Other into a world of persons, organisms and material objects united by their relations to one another . . . is, of course, the formal development of our primary *knowledge*. To consider it first has methodological advantages, but it is not without its dangers. For it may lead us back insensibly to that dualism of subject and object from which we are seeking to escape. It seems to presuppose an observer Self standing over against the Other and gradually differentiating the Object with increasing distinctness and clarity. We have, therefore, to remind ourselves now that knowledge is the negative dimension of action, and that a Self is primarily agent, and as such in active relation with the Other of which he forms part. Even if we confine our attention to the development of cognition in the child, we have to remember the mutuality of the personal relation which determines its form. Self and Other are correlatives, and the discrimination of the one involves a correlative discrimination of the other. If within the unity of the Other I discriminate personal, organic and material aspects, I discriminate these same aspects in myself. Moreover, in discriminating myself from the Other, it is always as belonging to the Other. The philosophical difficulty here we may leave unexplored until we come to discuss self-consciousness at a later stage.

[1]   From 'The Rhythm of Withdrawal and Return', *Persons in Relation* (London: Faber, 1961), pp. 86–105.

We must now, however, turn our attention to the positive
aspect of our personal development, that is to say to the development of the person as an agent, of which the development of the
capacity to discriminate the Other is merely the negative aspect.
We must consider the form of the development of the original system of motivation. For this purpose we must return to our
starting-point in the relation of mother and child. We have
noticed[2] how the periodic repetition of the normal acts of mothering — feeding, washing and so forth — sets up a rhythm of withdrawal and return within the relation. As the infant's capacity for
awareness increases, this rhythmic recurrence of the mother's
attentions will, we must presume, establish itself in the child's
consciousness as expectation based upon memory, and so provide the beginnings of knowledge. We are justified in using the
term knowledge at this early stage, because the reference to the
Other is, as we have seen, implicit from the beginning, and must
become explicit so soon as the necessary skills in discrimination
and correlating sensory and motor experiences are present. The
remembered response of the mother to his cries is expected to
repeat itself at regular intervals. Now this involves a number of
fundamental lessons to be learned. The first is learning to wait for
the response to his appeal. The second is learning to know the
Other as the repetition of the same, a lesson which underlies all
recognition of order and form. This is the reason why a regular
and invariant routine in the care of the young is of such importance; and it is the source of the child's demand for an invariant
repetition of what he is familiar with in a story or a game.

But this learning to wait and to expect has an even more fundamental bearing upon the development of motivation. The child's
recognition of a need for the mother to do something for him is
negatively motived. The persistence of this need, since he can do
nothing for its satisfaction, is accompanied by a growing discomfort and anxiety. Learning to wait for the right time involves,
therefore, the subordination of this negative motive to a positive
attitude of confidence that the expected response will come in due
time. This trust in the Other does not dispose of the discomfort or
the need. The negative motive remains operative; but the sting is
taken out of it by its integration in a complex attitude that is, as a

---

[2]   *Supra*, Chap. III, p. 76.

whole, positively determined. The expectation of the coming satisfaction can indeed be enjoyed, as men deliberately undertake and enjoy the dangers and labours and discomforts of climbing Mount Everest, in the expectation of achievement. So the infant's expectation is grounded in imagination; and his waiting is filled with the symbolic satisfaction of his desire in phantasy; the images he forms and the feelings of anticipatory pleasure which accompany them persist through the period of waiting, and coalesce, as it were, with the actual satisfaction when it comes. This exercising of the power of phantasy is the first stage in the development of reflection, and the succession of anticipation and satisfaction — with the same images accompanying both — institutes the primary distinction between imagining and perceiving.

But this state of positive motivation differentiated by the negative motive it contains and dominates depends upon the constant fulfilment of the expectation at the proper time. The expectation is, in fact, a prediction based on experience and constantly verified. But the unexpected may happen; the prediction may not be verified. Then the basis of confidence and security is broken. If the response to his cry is too long delayed, or if the mother's effort to relieve his distress is unsuccessful, then the negative motive is no longer subordinated to a positive, confident expectation. It becomes dominant, and finds expression in a paroxysm of rage and terror, and what power of phantasy the child has acquired will lend itself to the symbolic representation of danger.

In the earliest stage of our life this reversal of the natural dominance of the positive motive is occasional and accidental. It foreshadows however a periodic reversal which is necessary and inevitable in passing from one stage to the next. If a child is to grow up, he must learn, stage by stage, to do for himself what has up to that time been done for him by the mother. But at all the crucial points, at least, the decision rests with the mother, and therefore it must take the form of a deliberate refusal on her part to continue to show the child those expressions of her care for him that he expects. This refusal is, of course, itself an expression of the mother's care for him. But the child's stock of knowledge is too exiguous, the span of his anticipation too short, for him to understand this. For him, the refusal can only mean the breakdown of the relationship by which and in which he has his being. In his need he calls to the Other, but the Other is deaf to his entreaty. He is thrown back upon himself. His world has collapsed into irrationality; for the order in his experience of the Other is recurrence without change, the continuous repetition of identity. The constants of his experience of the world have disappeared; his anticipations have not been verified. His predictions are still, as it were, dogmas; he has not yet learned to treat them as hypotheses. The formula of his confidence is 'this or nothing'. So he faces what is for him the ultimate threat to his existence — isolation from the Other by the act of the Other.

The necessary consequence of such a situation is that the motivation system of the child's behaviour is thrown into reverse. The negative pole becomes dominant. Activity becomes egocentric, concerned with the defence of himself in a world which is indifferent to his needs, a world which acts in mysterious ways of its own, paying no attention to his desires. The emotional tone of such a phase of experience is one of anxiety; a general anxiety which, if it were to become permanent, must pass into despair. It is, of course, mitigated and qualified in various ways. For the positive motives remain active, though in subordination, differentiating the behaviour, and instigating an effort to overcome the negation and to restore the normal dominance of the positive. One aspect of this is that there is a positive pleasure for the child in acquiring and exercising the skill to do for himself what the mother refuses any longer to do for him. But it is important to recognize that this and other mitigating factors cannot of themselves provide a solution; that there is in fact no way in which the child can save himself from the anxiety which besets him. For the problem concerns the personal relation between himself and his mother: the anxiety is the fear that his mother does not love him any more, and he depends upon the mother while she does not depend upon him, at least in the same sense. He must indeed make an effort if there is to be a restoration of the mutual confidence that has been broken; but this can only succeed through the action of the mother. For since it was by his mother's action that the child's confidence was broken, it is only by her action that this confidence can be restored. If we may use the language of mature human reflection which, though its content is much richer, has an identical form, the child can only be rescued from his despair by the grace of the mother; by a revelation of her continued love and care which convinces him that his fears are groundless.

In this fashion there is established that rhythm of withdrawal and return which constitutes the universal and necessary pattern of personal development. Our immediate interest lies in its empirical functioning in the child's growth to maturity. But its importance is so great that we should first consider the pattern in its universal aspect, as a pure and necessary form. To do this we must consider the complete cycle, from the positive through the negative back to the positive, as ideally complete. This perfect achievement of the transition is, as we shall see, hardly to be expected in empirical experience. The overcoming of the negative always remains problematical.

The rhythm of withdrawal and return is the full dynamic expression of the form of the personal, as a positive which includes, is constituted by and subordinates its own negative. It is a succession of positive and negative phases which, taken together, constitutes the unity of a personal experience. The negative phase, therefore, depends upon, and is subordinate to, the positive, and the whole activity can only be defined through the positive. The negative, as we have seen, has meaning only by reference to the positive, and is therefore, as a phase of activity, for the sake of the positive. The withdrawal is for the sake of the return; and its necessity lies in this, that it differentiates the positive phase by enriching its content. Without the negative there could be no development of the positive, but only the repetition *ad infinitum* of an original undifferentiated identity.

Now the original unity which is developed in this way is a relation of persons. It is the unity of a common life. The 'You and I' relation, we must recall, constitutes the personal, and both the 'You' and the 'I' are constituted, as individual persons, by the mutuality of their relation. Consequently, the development of the individual person is the development of his relation to the Other. Personal individuality is not an original given fact. It is achieved through the progressive differentiation of the original unity of the 'You and I'. If this sounds difficult or paradoxical, it is yet a commonplace in some of its manifestations. We all distinguish ourselves, as individuals, from the society of which we are members and to which we belong. The paradox is the same: for we at once assert ourselves as constituent members of the society while opposing it to ourselves as the 'other-than-I'. So the child discovers himself as an individual by contrasting himself, and indeed by wilfully opposing himself, to the family *to which he belongs*; and this *discovery* of his individuality is at the same time the *realization* of his individuality. We are part of that from which we distinguish ourselves and to which, as agents, we oppose ourselves. In this — which is, indeed, simply another manifestation of the form of the personal — we may find the answer to many of the questions which puzzle the moralist; the existence of conscience, for example, of responsibility and the moral struggle; or, more generally, of the capacity which is possessed by a person, and only by a person, to represent his fellows — to feel and think and act, not for himself but for the other.

The difficulty we feel arises mainly because we are accustomed to think from the standpoint of reflection, and not of action. Persons are agents; and the relation of persons is a relation of agents, and in general is a *conditio sine qua non* of action. Without the support of a resistance there can be no action; and the resistance must, as we recognized,[3] be the resistance of a personal Other. Consequently, both the relation itself and the rhythm of its development are not merely matter of fact, though necessarily including matter of fact. They are matter of intention. Thus the negative phase, just as much as the positive, falls within the relation and presupposes it even while negating it. My withdrawal from the Other is itself a phase of my relation to the Other. The isolation of the self does not annul the relation; but refuses it. And since the relation is practical — since it is a relation of agents — the refusal is a practical activity which *intends* the annulment of the relation which it presupposes. There is here a radical contradiction in action. Since any personal relation enters into the constitution of the persons whom it relates, to annul the relation is to annul oneself, and to achieve the intention could only mean to destroy oneself along with the other. But further, the relation itself is not mere matter of fact, but matter of intention. To annul it, therefore, must mean not merely to bring it to an end as matter of fact; it must mean to annul the intention, and therefore the action, which constitutes it. Now time is the form of action, and consequently to annul the action implies a

---

[3]   *The Self as Agent*, p. 145.

reversal of the past. But this is impossible. The most we can do is, as we sometimes say, to make it *as if* it had never been. The most that such negative relation in action can achieve is a *symbolic* annulment; the appearance but not the reality of annulment.

Consider, as an example, the following situation. An only son has publicly disgraced his family. His father, bitterly affected by the disgrace, decides that he will have no more to do with the fellow and publicly disowns him. He disinherits his son, erases his name from the family record, refuses to see him, and cuts him 'dead' if he meets him by accident. If anyone refers to his son in his presence, he replies with a stony emphasis, 'I have no son'. In such a case the relation of father and son remains a fact, and the father is perfectly aware of this. Indeed, his behaviour presupposes the fact. He insists he has no son because he knows, and the people to whom he speaks also know, and know that he knows that he has. The non-existence of his son is thus not matter of fact, but matter of intention; but this intention is unrealizable, since it could only be realized by altering the past. It is not sufficient to say that he wishes his son were dead; it would be truer to say that he wishes his son had never been born. But even this is not a satisfactory diagnosis, for a wish is not an intention, and he behaves deliberately as though the facts were other than they are. He might, of course, kill his son, but that would be no solution. For what he intends to annul is not his son's future, and not merely his son's past, but his own past in having a son and caring for him. His behaviour can only be symbolic. Even if he were to kill his son and then himself, his action would be merely symbolic. It would symbolize, in a particular case, what is here asserted as a general principle, that the positive personal relation with his son is for him the sole intrinsic good, so that when this is negated in intention, it becomes impossible for him to intend his own existence, or that of his son.

There is always an element of illusion associated with the negative phase in the rhythm of personal development. This, indeed, is one aspect of its negativity. In the case of the child whose mother refuses to satisfy his expectation any longer, it *appears* that she refuses any longer to care for him; yet in reality her refusal is itself an expression of her continuing care for him. The illusion is necessary. The refusal throws his world into chaos. For it is the household routine, not the orderly succession of the seasons, which guarantees for the child the 'uniformity of nature'. The failure of the repetition of the same in his mother's care for him is to him what the failure of the sun to rise in due course would be for us. For him as for us, the possibility of life depends upon the faith that the future will be as the past, that we have a right to believe in the fulfilment of expectations based upon past experience. But expectation is relative to experience. We have learned that the constants we have found in experience may not represent the structure of reality in general; but hold only within a limited range of experience, as special cases of wider constancies. We have learned that the order of the world is more complex than our knowledge of it had led us to believe. We have learned, in science, that all our generalizations are hypothetical, that our best grounded predictions are provisional; we have even learned to see the search for the falsification of our expectations as the surest path to a wider knowledge of the world. The child is only beginning to learn this; and what he is learning is the distinction between appearance and reality. It is necessary that the mother should refuse him what he has every reason to expect; it is necessary that within the relationship with her he should be forced into negativity, believe that she has ceased to care for him and be afraid. For only so can he experience the distinction between positive and negative in its fundamental manifestations; as the distinction between real and unreal, between good and evil, beautiful and ugly, true and false. For all of us, at any stage, development depends upon the rhythm of withdrawal and return; and this is true for societies as for individuals. If the rhythm ceases, development ceases with it, and we are ripe for death or for destruction.

This will become clearer if we notice another characteristic of the negative phase of the personal relation — its egocentricity. To be negatively motivated is to be concerned for oneself in relation to the Other. The relation cannot be annulled; and the reference to the Other, since it is constitutive for the personal, cannot be evaded. We need the Other in order to be ourselves. But in any relation, the focus of attention and interest may become centred upon Self rather than on the Other; and since this is brought about through the refusal of the Other to respond to my need — or what appears to me to be my need — my negative attitude defines the

Other as a danger to myself. This egocentric attitude has often been referred to as 'self-love', through failure to draw the distinction between positive and negative motivation. Self-love is self-contradictory. Love is necessarily for the Other, and self-love would mean self-alienation. But fear of the Other is fear for oneself, and involves a concentration of interest and activity upon the defence of the Self. The role of the negative phase in the development of the personal relation is therefore the development of individuality. It is the phase of self-assertion, self-consciousness and self-development, in opposition to the Other. Its general ideal, which necessarily contains an element of illusion, is independence of the Other and self-sufficiency.

The child, at any of the critical stages of his early development, when forced into the negative phase by the mother's refusal to do for him any longer what he has come to expect will, *in fact*, learn to do it for himself. He will, *as a matter of fact*, grow up and come to play the part required of him, stage by stage, until he reaches the independence of maturity. But this does not mean that he has developed satisfactorily, and even the skill and capacity which he shows in his adult occupations, whether of body or mind, is an inadequate measure of the success of his education. For these are functional — and therefore negative — aspects of his personal life, and the defining, positive aspect is his relation to the Other, and at the centre of this his relation to other persons. His quality as a person is the quality of his personal relations; and since a person is an agent, this means the character of the persistent system of motives which determines his personal relations. The formal aspect of this is the question whether his activities are in general negatively or positively motivated, and it is this question upon which we must concentrate our attention.

The mother's refusal of what he expects from her confronts the child with a contradiction in his consciousness, which has various aspects. The primary aspect is practical, as a clash of wills. Hitherto, his expectation has been regularly fulfilled. He has learned to expect, that is, to imagine in advance, to refer a present symbol to a future occurrence. Now he goes on imagining a future which does not occur and the longer it is postponed the greater becomes his fear and the more vivid his expectation. The expectation, persistently unfulfilled, becomes a demand. His cry for what he

expects passes into an angry insistence, even perhaps into a paroxysm of rage. This is the genesis of will, which always implies a
self-assertion against the Other, an opposition to be overcome,
and therefore an awareness of Self as opposed to the Other. This
conflict of wills individualizes the child for himself; and the
mother who opposes him, for him. He recognizes himself as an
agent through the opposition of another agent, who seeks to
determine his future against his own will.

This exposition should not be taken as determining a particular
point in a child's development at which self-consciousness super-
venes upon a consciousness of an earlier kind. It is to be taken generally and diagrammatically. The distinction of Self and Other is
present from the beginning, since the infant, being dependent
totally upon the mother, must wait upon the other person for the
satisfaction of his needs. There is a necessary time lag between the
consciousness of need and its satisfaction. But so long as the
expectation is not disappointed, so long as there is a regularity in
the recurrence of the supply of his needs, there is no crisis which
concentrates attention upon himself by compelling him to make a
demand instead of merely waiting passively. At most there is a
point in personal development, which may vary considerably from
child to child, at which the contrast between Self and Other is
finally established as a pervasive attitude in action and reflection.

The negative aspect of this contradiction in consciousness establishes the reflective distinction between good and bad, and
between true and false. The mother's refusal institutes a dichotomy
in the child's consciousness between what he expects and what
actually occurs; between his demand and the response to it. He is
forced into a recognition of the distinction between imagining and
perceiving. For what he anticipates in imagination is contradicted
by what actually takes place, and this institutes the contrast
between phantasy and reality. But here we must remember that
this happens in action and that the Other is personal. Both sides of
the distinction are referred to the Other. What is imagined is what
is demanded of the Other. What occurs is something distinct from
what is demanded, which the Other actually does. The contrast of
what is imagined with what is perceived is an aspect of the conflict
of wills. It is indeed the knowledge of this conflict. The distinction
between what is imagined and what is perceived represent, in the

consciousness of the individual, the contradiction between his own will and the will of the Other; between what he intends that the Other should do and what the Other intends and does. To recognize this distinction is to recognize one's own frustration.

Now what the child expects the mother to do is what, relatively to his knowledge, would satisfy his need. It is, then, what she ought to do, but will not. So his mother is wicked. In his fear for himself he is angry with her and hates her. Yet this hate and anger depend upon his need of her love, and his memory of the time when he and she loved one another. Moreover, the situation in which he finds himself, and the state of mind into which he is come, is one which is dreadful to him and from which he needs to escape. Yet he can only escape from it, it appears to him, if she will change her mind, and be good to him again. Then he will forgive her and they will be reconciled: they will be friends again and enjoy one another.

Within this contradiction of will and feeling the purely factual distinction between true and false is contained. For there is in it a conception of the order of the world, however simple and unaffirmed, and an expectation based upon that conception, which has proved false in the event. This distinction, however, is still implicit; it is derivative and subordinate. For the Other is personal, and the order of events on which memory bases expectation is the past actions of the mother in caring for her child. The personal relation is primarily practical. His mother has played him false by acting wrongly. We have seen that the distinction between right and wrong is inherent in the nature of action.[4] We see now that this distinction, without which there can be no action, but only reaction to stimulus, is involved in the original structure of human motivation; and that it has its ultimate moral reference through the personal relation which constitutes the human individual a person. What we are here considering is the origin of the moral struggle, in a situation which is universal and necessary in human experience. This situation is the conflict of wills between mother and child. The moral struggle is primarily a struggle between persons. It is only secondarily, though also necessarily, a struggle within the individual. For the motivation of the individual and the consciousness which it contains, has refer-

[4]   *The Self as Agent*, p. 140.

ence to the Other. He needs the Other in order to be himself; and his awareness is an awareness of the Other. Consequently, if his relation to the Other becomes negative, the conflict is reflected in himself. He must maintain the relation even in rejecting it: he cannot escape from it except by escaping from himself. His relation to the Other becomes ambivalent. He is divided in himself, fearing and therefore hating what he loves, turned against himself because he is against the Other. From this conflict of agents are derived all the characteristic dichotomies in terms of which human life must be lived, and in it they are contained. With their emergence in consciousness, as distinctions between real and unreal, right and wrong, good and evil, true and false, action becomes necessary and human life becomes problematic. We are compelled to distinguish and to choose.

These reflections upon the formal structure of the moment of withdrawal in personal development do not merely disclose the origin of the ultimate distinctions which make human life problematic. They reveal the form of the basic problem itself. In its largest scope it is the problem of reconciliation. From the standpoint of the individual it is the problem of overcoming fear. Think once again of the child's situation. He is refused what experience has given him the right to expect, and his cosmos has returned to chaos. He is obliged to do something for himself which his mother has always done for him. His mother compels him to do it. But we must notice that this compulsion is not a physical compulsion. It is in the nature of things impossible to compel another person to act, if by compulsion we mean a merely physical necessitation. The capacity to act is freedom. The most we can do is to provide another with a sufficient motive for doing what we want him to do. The motive, however, may be negative. We may make him afraid not to do what we demand of him. The child is in this case. His need for his mother is absolute; his fear for himself refers to this need for the mother's care. Consequently, he has a sufficient motive for doing what she requires, however much against his will.

Now if this is what happens; if the child learns to do what is required of him for fear of the consequences to himself, he has failed to make the return to a positive motivation from the negative phase of withdrawal. The negative motive remains dominant. He is still on the defensive. He has indeed returned to the field of action; but he acts from negative, and, therefore, egocentric motives. He has learned to do something for himself, but for his own sake; and his individual character is by that much more negative.

If the return from the negative phase is to be completely successful it is necessary that the dominance of the negative motive be completely overcome, and that the positive relation to the mother be fully re-established, in spite of her continuing refusal to satisfy his demand. It is the conditions and implications of such a successful overcoming of fear that concern our study. We may sum them up by saying that they consist in recognizing the illusions involved in the negative phase, and as a consequence the disappearance of the conflict of wills. This recognition of illusion does not necessarily involve its expression in judgment, and in the earliest stage of our development it cannot do so. To recognize as unreal what has been taken as real is to reverse a valuation, and value, we have seen,[5] is primarily felt. The 'facts' of the situation remain unchanged. What is required for the recognition of unreality is a change of feeling from negative to positive (or vice versa), coupled with a memory of the earlier attitude.

The judgment which would express the child's attitude in the negative phase is this. 'Mother doesn't love me any more'; or, as it hardens into definiteness and arouses the will, 'Mother is against me'. It is this feeling that constitutes the negative relation of persons, and is therefore mutual. 'If Mother is against me then I am against her'. Now to overcome this negation, it is necessary that the judgment should be reversed, and its reversal involves the recognition that it was illusory. The further judgment must be 'Mother appeared to be against me, but she wasn't really'. This primary recognition of the distinction between appearance and reality carries certain fundamental implications, however long it may take a child to recognize them fully. Of these, we may notice two which are of fundamental formal significance. The first is the implication that he was wrong; that his feeling, and so his valuation, of the Other, was mistaken. We might formulate this by saying, 'I thought Mother was bad, but she wasn't. She was good. It was I who was bad'. This provides the formal basis of moral experience. The second implication provides the basis of intellectual

---

[5]   *The Self as Agent*, p. 190.

experience — the distinction between true and false. The child
recognizes in action, if not yet in reflection, that his expectation
was based upon too limited an experience. His conception of the
'uniformity of Nature' — as we are used to calling the repetition
of the same — was too simple. What appeared to be constants
have turned out to be variables. Thus the disappointment of
expectation based upon the experience of an invariant sequence
in the behaviour of the Other provides the experience of being in
error. But with regard to this implication, we must note that it is
relatively independent of the pattern of motivation and the
rhythm of its changes. Whether the child succeeds or fails in overcoming the negation in his relation to the mother he must recognize that his expectation has been falsified. Here he is dealing
with mere matter of fact. For this reason our knowledge of the
impersonal aspect of our world is always relatively independent
of our feelings, attitudes and motives. I say 'relatively' because
the activities through which we gain such knowledge can never
be independent of the motives which sustain them. These
motives, though they may have little relevance to the truth or falsity of the conclusions we reach, still determine the direction of
our attention; and so the kind of questions we ask, to which our
conclusions are the answers

The return from the negative is not, then, necessarily achieved
in its completeness, or satisfactorily. If it were, the original positive relation of mother and child would be re-established fully at a
higher level; a level at which the child has learned to trust the
mother in spite of appearances, and at which he has something to
contribute of his own initiative to the common life. Instead of
doing what he has learned to do for himself, from fear of the consequences, he would do it for the mother, in co-operation with
her, and so as an expression of their mutual affection. The critical
evidence of such a satisfactory return to full positive mutuality
would be the complete disappearance in the child of any desire
for the earlier stage which he has out-grown, of any hankering
after more infantile expressions of affection. But such a success is
beyond the bounds of all probability, at least as a continuing
achievement in all the repetitions of the rhythm of withdrawal
and return which make up the personal development to maturity.
It may be achieved, or nearly achieved, upon occasion, but on the

whole and on balance the most we can hope for is a qualified success. The main reason for this lies in the mother. A complete success would only be possible if the mother's relation to the child was and remained continuously fully positive and free from egocentricity. Her task in the development is to convince the child without going back upon her refusal to give him what he demands, that his fear that she is against this is an illusion; and that she refuses what he wants wholly for his sake, and not at all for her own. Even with the best of mothers this can be so only in the main, and never absolutely and continuously. So far as she falls short of this perfection of love, so far the child's feeling that she is against him is not an illusion; and by so much she must fail to overcome his negative attitude and to reinstate a fully positive relation.

Finally, then, we must consider the formal result of this general failure to overcome completely the negative motivation which sustains the phase of withdrawal, and consequently the illusions and contradictions which are inseparable from it. The failure must mean that the relation with the Other at the higher level is established upon a mixed motive. It contains an element of fear which is not integrated within the positive motivation of the return to action, but suppressed. This suppression is possible through a concentration of attention. The intention of an action, as we saw,[6] is bound up with the attention which selects the field of our awareness in acting. But no action can have contradictory intentions. We cannot aim in different directions at the same time. It can, however, have contradictory motives, one of which is suppressed, and therefore 'unconscious'. And since our actions contain a negative element which is in the same sense 'unconscious', the unconscious motive may find expression in action, so that we find that what we have done is not what we intended, but something different; even something opposite and contradictory to our intention. In our relations with other persons this ambiguity of motivation is felt as a tension and a constraint between us, and therefore in each of us.

For simplicity's sake let us return to the child, and consider only the extreme possibilities. In the phase of withdrawal he is obsessed by an unfulfilled expectation, which persists as a

---

[6]   *The Self as Agent*, pp. 171 f.

demand for its fulfilment. But he is faced with a demand from his mother which is incompatible with his own demand. His need for the mother is such that he needs must accede to her demand, and so accept, in practice, the new phase of active co-operation with her. In this return to co-operation, if the negative motive which sustains his own demand is fully overcome, the demand itself will disappear, the desire which sustains it will cease to operate, and he will find a full satisfaction in the new mode of relationship. The conflict between imagination and actuality — between his image of what should occur, and what actually does occur — is fully resolved. If, on the contrary, he accedes to his mother's demand because he must, and against his will, the tension of contradiction is not resolved. He remains egocentric and on the defensive; he conforms in behaviour to what is expected of him, but, as it were, as a matter of policy. In that case, he cannot find satisfaction in the new forms of co-operation, and they remain for him unreal. His heart is not in them. Consequently, the desire, and the activity of imagination which it sustains, do not disappear. The contradiction between the imagined satisfaction and the unsatisfactory actual persists. If this condition becomes habitual by repetition — and it must tend to do so, because the earlier experiences of withdrawal and return tend to become models for those that follow — it will institute a permanent dualism between the ideal and the actual, which will be accepted by the negatively motivated individual as normal. Here, then, is an account to the genesis of dualism as a habit of mind.

The child who has been forced back into co-operative activity without a resolution of the conflict has two courses open to him. He remains egocentric, and the objective of his behaviour is security, through self-defence. What he cannot do, so long as his fear is not overcome and dissipated, is to give himself freely to his mother in the fellowship of mutual affection without constraint. The conflict remains. He can either run away or fight. If he takes the first course, he will conform obediently and even eagerly to the pattern of behaviour expected of him. He will become a 'good' boy, and by his 'goodness' he will seek to placate the mother whose enmity he fears. In compensation for this submission he will create for himself a secret life of phantasy where his own wishes are granted. And this life of the imagination in an imaginary world will be for him his *real* life in the *real* world — the world of ideas. His life in the actual world will remain unreal — a necessity which he will make as habitual and automatic as possible. What importance it has for him will derive from its necessity as a support for and a means to his real life, which is the life of thought, the spiritual life, the life of the mind.

He may, however, take the other course. He may seek to impose his own will upon his mother. He may become a 'bad' boy, rebellious and aggressive, seeking to gain by force or cunning what is not freely given to him. In that case he will carry the conflict of wills into the world of actuality, and seek power over the Other. He will use his imagination to discover and exploit the weaknesses of those on whom he is dependent, and to devise techniques for getting his own way. The frustration of his aggressiveness and the penalties of his disobedience will then increase his hostility, and with it his efforts to find the power and the means to assert his own will successfully and to compel compliance with his demands. *His* real life is the practical life, the life of action as the use of power to secure his own ends by his own efforts. The life of the imagination is unreal in itself, and has value for him only as a means to success in the practical life.

When this failure to overcome the negative motivation is established, one or other of these two courses will tend to become habitual by repetition. Through this process — which is the critical centre of all education — there will be produced an individual who is either characteristically submissive or characteristically aggressive in his active relation with the Other. This contrast of types of disposition corresponds to the distinction drawn by psychologists between the 'introvert' and the 'extravert'. But because we are drawing the distinction for philosophical purposes, we must do more than accept an empirical classification. In particular, we must understand their relation to one another as aspects of the form of the personal. I must draw attention, therefore, in summary fashion, to a few major implications of the analysis.

These two modes of behaviour are ambivalent. They have the same motive and the same ultimate objective — fear for oneself in relation to the Other, and the defence of oneself against the threat from the Other. They are, therefore, ambivalent forms of negative or egocentric behaviour. No individual can conform fully to either type; and the same individual will on occasion exchange the one mode of defence for the other. The two type forms are, therefore, better regarded as extreme limits between which fall the actual dispositions of human beings; each one varying its place from time to time within these limits while having a place on the scale which is, on the whole, its characteristic position.

Secondly, both types of attitude — submissive and aggressive — are negative, and therefore involve unreality. They carry over the illusion of the negative phase of withdrawal into the return to active relationship. They motivate a behaviour in relationship which is contradictory, and, therefore, self-defeating. For the inherent objective — the reality of the relationship — is the full mutuality of fellowship in a common life, in which alone the individual can realize himself as a person. But both the dispositions are egocentric, and motivate action which is for the sake of oneself, and not for the sake of the Other; which is, therefore, self-interested. Such action is implicitly a refusal of mutuality, and an effort to constrain the Other to do what we want. By conforming submissively to his wishes we put him under an obligation to care for us. By aggressive behaviour we seek to make him afraid not to care for us. In both cases, we are cheating; and in both cases the Other is compelled to defend himself against our deception, even though it is a self-deception. Self-interested relation excludes the mutuality it seeks to exhort. If it succeeds in its intention, it produces the appearance of mutuality, not the reality. It can produce, at most, a reciprocity of co-operation which simulates, even while it excludes, the personal unity which it seeks to achieve.

Finally, these two negative dispositions, however persistent they may be, are never unalterable. For they are not innate characters, but habits which have been learned. In principle, what has been learned can be unlearned; and empirical experience offers us many examples of the transformation of character, sometimes by a gradual change, sometimes by a sudden and dramatic conversion. The rhythm of withdrawal and return does not cease with the achievement of organic maturity; it is the permanent form of life of personal relationship. The transition from the withdrawal to the return repeats itself indefinitely, and each time it is made there is a possibility that it should be made successfully.

Six

The Conception of Society

The social character of human life has been so long emphasized by writers of all schools of thought that it has become engrained in our minds. We all admit readily that in some sense society is of the essence of humanity, however we differ about the conclusions to be drawn there-from. Aristotle's bold assertion that 'man is a social animal' has taken on for us the form and habit of an axiom, though it may be doubted whether the old Greek's meaning, that the desire to live a private life of one's own is evidence of psychological abnormality, if of nothing worse, would not meet with hot denial from many quarters, especially from that type of Englishman whose home is his castle. In some sense, too, the axiom is undoubtedly valid. Society *is* essential to humanity. Not merely does the fact that we live together, in constant relation to one another, determine and limit our individual activity in countless ways, but if we could in imagination abstract the social element from human experience, with it would have to go whatever is distinctively human, and indeed rationality itself. For speech, which is a social phenomenon, is inseparable from the use and the development of reason.

Yet here, as always in philosophy, a superficial agreement may hide an underlying difference of opinion. In agreeing about the social character of human life each of us interprets the phrase in his own fashion, and what may seem at first sight a very slight shade of difference may, when its implications have worked

[1]   From 'The Conception of Society', *Proceedings of the Aristotelian Society*, 31 (1930–1), pp. 127–42.

themselves out, reveal divergencies not merely of theoretical importance, but of great practical moment as well. It seems worth while, therefore, to consider what we mean by 'society', and to attempt to rid the term of ambiguity. For, as used in modern philosophy, and in particular by modern idealists, the term has a vagueness associated with it which is inimical to clear thinking, and which indeed serves to cast a protective haze over theories which dare not face the clear light of analysis.

When we consider the common usage of the term 'society' we can distinguish in it two conceptions between which it varies, and from the confusion of which its ambiguity arises. When we say that human nature is inherently social, we may mean either that every human being is a member of some group of human beings, or we may mean that human nature can only manifest itself through intercourse between human beings. The first of these conceptions refers society to the phenomena of group-life, and involves a contrast between the individual and society, society in that case being the group to which the individual belongs. For this reason I propose to call it the *substantival* conception of society. In this sense of the term, society is an entity, so that we can say that we are all members of society and society can be asserted or denied to possess rights and claims against the individual. In contrast to this, the second conception may be called *adjectival*, since it makes society a characteristic or property of human life, or perhaps rather a quality of human life. In this sense society must be contrasted not with the individual, but rather with solitariness. It is this conception of society which lies behind the use of the term in the phrase 'enjoying the society of one's fellows', or in Byron's well-known line, 'There is society where none intrudes'. This adjectival conception of society, which one might perhaps define as the mutuality of human life, has been so overborne in scientific and philosophical discussion by the substantial conception, that some recent writers have suggested the revival of the old word 'sociality' to take its place. At first sight it might seem that these conceptions of society were not antithetical, but merely different aspects of one and the same conception. It is the contention of this paper that this is not so; that if we develop the implications of each they turn out to be in important respects antithetical.

Let us look first at the implications of the substantival conception. This conception is solidly rooted in the fact that human beings have always tended to live in groups, and in groups which have a sufficient permanence and sufficient unity to be distinguished as separate units and identified by persistent characteristics. Now if a collection of human beings is to be a group, it must have some kind of unity of its own. It must have some inherent structure in it which makes a real whole, so that it behaves as a single entity and not as a mere number of individuals who happen, accidentally, to be together. Any composite whole, consisting of existent individuals, is a whole in virtue of some objective principle of unification inherent in it which unites these individuals, and the group-entity is the individuals so united. We must distinguish between a group and a class. A class of entities is not necessarily a group. Entities form a class in virtue of some property that is exhibited in each member of the class: they are particulars which can be subsumed under the same universal. But entities form a group in virtue of some principle of cohesion between them which unites them as individuals so that they act as one. A group is an existent whose members are individual existents. But even if the members of a class are all existents, the class itself is not. Thus all men are members of the class human beings, but there is no group which consists of all human beings. It is conceivable that in the future all living human beings should form a single group, or a single society, but it would not be because each individual was a human being, but because some principle of cohesion which is now absent had appeared which unified them so that they had come to form a real whole.

Now, since a group is a composite existent whose members are real individuals, it must be finite. There must be limits to its inclusiveness. At any one time it must consist of so many members and no more, and any individual either is or is not a member of the group. The same individual may, of course, at one time be a member and at another not a member; and the number of the members may vary from time to time. But since a group is an actual entity it exists only as an actual cohesion of an actual number of individuals. It is a group just in so far as its members do actually cohere and exhibit a solidarity of behaviour. If then society is the fact of group life, it must manifest itself in the actual existence of cohesive groups of human beings, and if society is essential to human life, all human beings must belong to some group of human beings which is actually unified.

Moreover, no individual can be a member of two groups at the same time, unless one of the groups includes the other as a sub-group within it. An individual can, of course, be a member of two different classes at the same time, since he can be classified in terms of different properties or characteristics which he possesses. But to be a member of a group he must be united, as a concrete individual, with other individuals, and form part of an actual composite whole. For this reason, he can no more be a part of two groups at the same time than a wheel can be the wheel of two bicycles at the same time. His actual membership of a group is his actual partnership in the activity of the group as an entity.

On the substantival conception of society, society is conceived as an entity, and therefore as a group of human beings. An individual is, therefore, a member of society by being a member of a particular group of human beings, and *not* a member of any other, unless that other group is a sub-group of the first. His nature as a social being is the fact that he behaves as a member of such a group, and not of any other. He may, of course, at one time be a member of one group and at another time of another group: but he cannot be simultaneously a member of both. The unity of society, on this view, is the actual fact of its solidarity. The principle of unity which binds its members into a group is an actual and active force. If it is not, then there is no actual group.

It will be objected, no doubt, that this is not true of human society as we know it. The same individual may, for example, be a member of the Roman Catholic Church, of an international group of scientists, and of the French nation; and none of these groups includes the others. This is undoubtedly true, and it is, perhaps, a fatal objection to the conception of society which we are examining. But for the moment, let us waive this point and consider one or two others. Unless society is an actual group exhibiting *de facto* solidarity, any attempt to contrast the individual and society will be logically vicious. The individual is undeniably an actual entity, and unless society is equally an actual entity, the opposition is not *in pari materia*, and the conclusions which are the result of disregarding this will be invalid. Now a very great deal of our social and political philosophy does depend upon this contrast of society and the individual, in the form which demands that society shall be thought of as an actual entity. Whenever we discuss the relations of society to the individual, or assign authority to society, or refer to the will or the conscience or the power of society, we imply that society is an entity, a real existent, even if we do not go so far as to call it a group-person. If society is not an entity, then all such discussions simply confuse the issue; and if they are valid at all, society must be an actual entity, with the characteristics which we have seen.

This is the reason, it seems to me, why any social philosophy which implies that society is an actual group-entity cannot avoid the confusion between society and the State. It can, of course, distinguish between the community as the group-unity of persons and the State as the legal and governmental organization which is the political aspect of the community. But this is not the point. What it cannot do is to avoid defining the limits of the social entity in terms of citizenship. For the political organization is the only definite, persistent and actual principle of unification which can determine society as an actual group-entity in the proper sense. Only if we can make the membership of the State define the limits of a particular society, can we secure for our thought a content which approximates to that inclusiveness and exclusiveness which the substantival conception of society demands. Any theory which contrasts the individual and society, or the individual and the group, or the individual and the community, however carefully it distinguishes between society and the State, is driven to mean by society or community or group, the particular body of persons which is determined by a common citizenship.

Two very practical consequences may be mentioned here. The substantival conception of society tends necessarily to support the effort of the State to make itself an inclusive power by assuming the right to control, as subordinate groupings of individuals, all other societies. That tendency has other sources, less theoretical; but the theory that is implied in the substantival conception of society strengthens and supports it. When we think of society as an entity we are impelled to find, and if we cannot find to construct, an entity which will correspond to it, and our only means of doing this is to construct a society on the basis of a common citizenship. The second consequence of importance is closely bound up with this. It is the idea of nationalism. For nationalism again is an effort to equate a society conceived as an entity — the nation — with the State, and so to provide a limit of political organization to the nexus of social relationships. There are undoubtedly practical reasons, as things are, for making, so far as conditions permit, the nation the unit of political organization. But so far as I can see, there are no valid theoretical grounds for doing so. Nationality is largely an historical accident of conditions in Western Europe, where the isolation produced by differences of language or geographical situation have tended to produce a limitation of social relationships which has corresponded with the limitations of the territory of a particular State. But there is no valid ground for suggesting that this state of things *ought* to be reproduced everywhere, or that a community of culture and so forth is the only valid ground for determining the proper unit of political organization. In effect, nationalism is always an effort of exclusion, aiming at giving definite limits to a community of social relationships, and so to produce a group-entity corresponding to the substantival conception of society.

But the very fact that such efforts have to be made to bring actual society into line with the substantival conception of it is in itself a proof that society is not an actual entity. At best it is an ideal entity, a conception of society which is to be realized, and to which actual society approximates or towards which it develops. The failure of the facts of modern social life to square with the substantival conception of society do in this manner drive its upholders into idealism. In spite of all Duguit's pleading, the nature of law, for example, cannot be based upon any actual fact of social solidarity. If the social solidarity of any State were actual, there would be no need of law. The citizens would act as one group-entity, and law could only be, at the most, a description of the actual unity the community possessed, not in any sense an instrument for the production of such a unity in action, nor a prescription of forms of common action which needed to be enforced. On the other hand, the moment we admit this, and recognize that social solidarity is an ideal, and society as a group-entity is not so much fact as something that is to be achieved, we find ourselves in another difficulty. The distinction between the individual and society is no longer *in pari materia*, since the individual is an actual entity and the society is not. All claims of society upon the individual are based upon the assumption that society is actual; and if society is not actual, then these claims fall to the ground. This is, in fact, the dilemma of all modern idealism in its political philosophy. It seeks to justify the obligations of the individual to society through a conception of society as an ideal entity, while the individual who is saddled with these obligations remains an actual individual. In Rousseau's phrase, it takes 'men as they are and States as they ought to be'. As a consequence it is continually involved in fruitless efforts to equate the society as an ideal entity with the society as an actual entity.

If, however, we ask ourselves under what conditions human society naturally tends to show itself as a group-entity, the answer is, under primitive conditions. Primitive societies do tend to be groups exhibiting an actual social solidarity, though this solidarity of the group is probably never so complete, even in the most primitive human life, as it is amongst the animals. The process of human development, indeed, is a process which breaks down this primitive solidarity of the tribe. It is the absence of any clear self-consciousness, the elementary state of that peculiarly human capacity for distinguishing oneself as an individual from other individuals, and therefore of acting as an individual, which produces in primitive society that approximation to the herd-life of animals, which makes human society express itself as a group-entity. The more civilization develops the less is this the case, and the more do social relationships cease to express themselves in the formation of group-entities.

We may now turn to the adjectival conception of society and try to develop its implications in turn. From this point of view, society is in no sense an entity, either actual or ideal. It is not a group of human beings. It is a characteristic quality of human experience which is realized in the intercourse of human beings. Whenever two or more persons enter into human relationships with one another there is society, and that society is not the group of persons so formed, nor is it the relationship between them, but a character of the experience they have in that relationship, its mutuality.

The fact from which this conception starts is the fact of the sharing of experience. All human experience is the experience of individual persons. The subject of experience is always an individual. Yet two persons may share the same experience, and share it consciously. That this is a fact cannot be denied without a relapse into Solipsism, and to discuss Solipsism is to deny it. The possibility of speech depends upon this sharing, and the possibility of any common knowledge. So does the possibility of self-consciousness, and therefore of reason itself. Indeed, it may well be argued that rationality, as commonly understood, is our aspect of society in this sense.

Now, this quality of experience, its mutuality, is necessarily a quality of *individual* experience, since all experience is the experience of individual persons. It is therefore impossible to contrast the experience of the individual with social experience, if by that is meant the experience of a society. The adjectival conception of society therefore implies that the contrast between the individual and society is radically false, and must vitiate any theory which is determined or conditioned by it. The consciousness of society is individual consciousness; it is, in fact, the consciousness of a commonness in my individual experience, so that, though my experience is wholly mine, it is not merely mine.

To understand this we must consider the fact of objectivity, which is fundamental in our experience. Objectivity is in the true sense the capacity, which characterizes persons, of living in a world of objects. The phrase is instructive, and curious. It distinguishes us from the world, and yet places our life not in ourselves, but in the world from which we are distinguished. The world is the not-self, the object; yet we live not in the self, but in the world. We are most familiar with the discussion of objectivity in respect of knowledge. Knowing is a capacity of the self, but it is a grasping of that which is not self but object, a cognition of *its* nature: and it therefore presupposes the existence of what is known as a distinct entity, with a nature of its own, independent of the knower. The capacity to know is precisely this capacity to transcend the limits of the self and to live, in thought, by the nature of that which is not the self; to think in terms of a nature which lies beyond the limits of our own nature. This capacity for objectivity is not, however, confined to cognition. On the practical side it shows itself as the capacity to act in terms of the nature of the not-self; not therefore by impulse, by a determination from within, but objectively, by a determination through the nature of that which is external to us. The same is true of our emotional experience. There is a capacity for emotional objectivity, which is manifested at its highest in the great artists; a capacity to feel in terms of the nature of the world outside us and so to apprehend the value of that which is not ourselves.

This capacity for objectivity is the essential *differentia* of human experience. It is in virtue of its objectivity that it is human. What we are specially concerned with here is its relation to self-consciousness. It has often been pointed out, both by psychologists and philosophers, that self-consciousness is essentially relative to consciousness of the not-self. To be aware of myself is to distinguish myself from that which is not myself. To this we must add that the apprehended character of the self depends upon the apprehended character of the not-self from which it is distinguished. I apprehend myself as body in apprehending bodies in the external world. I apprehend myself as a living creature in distinction from living creatures in the world which are not myself. Similarly, I apprehend myself as a self, that is to say, as a person, only in and through the apprehension of other persons in the world who are not myself. Self-consciousness, in the full sense of the term, as consciousness of myself as a self, implies my consciousness of other persons as selves. But now, since to be conscious of my selfhood is to be conscious of my capacity for objectivity, it implies my consciousness of the same capacity in other persons. Thus, self-consciousness is essentially consciousness of myself as an object for other selves. This self-consciousness has of course its emotional and its practical aspects as well as its cognitional aspect. It involves sympathy and co-operation. In its completeness it is the unity of the three. But in all its aspects it implies a mutuality of experience. Self-consciousness is not that impossibility of the systems in which the isolated self is doubled back upon itself. It is the reflection of my own selfhood in the selfhood of another, who is at once object for me and subject for whom I am object. Self-consciousness and the experience of mutuality are thus two sides of the same penny; and so far as human consciousness is conditioned by self-consciousness, it is conditioned by a mutuality of experience between persons: or, to put it otherwise, so far as human consciousness is potentially self-conscious, it is potentially social.

We can now realize the sense in which, on the adjectival conception of society, human nature is essentially social. Because human experience is the consciousness of a person, it involves this quality of mutuality, of commonness. It is shared or shareable experience. Full personal objectivity is the capacity to live in a world of other persons, and so in terms of the reality and nature of other persons. Apart from this capacity, experience is not properly human, or, to use an old and misleading term, rational. Rational experience is inherently mutual experience, objective experience, common experience. Human society is not the fact of relationships between persons, but the consciousness of these relationships as a factor in the consciousness of the individuals so related. A set of actual relationships between a number of persons which rendered them mutually interdependent might constitute them a defined group, a State, for instance; but it would not constitute them a society. At least the consciousness of these relationships and of this interdependence in the minds of all the related individuals would be necessary and, indeed, more than this bare consciousness; for the realization of society involves the achievement of a real mutuality of shared experience. It is this that cuts at the root of all attempts to explain society in terms of instinctive gregariousness. A group maintained by instinctive tendencies is not a society. The disappearance of the instinct would in that case merely involve the disintegration of the group. But if a man becomes antisocial and retires into the solitude of a hermit's life his consciousness is still a social consciousness. He disapproves of society, he dislikes society, he refuses to enter into relations with other men. But he is still conscious of society, and carries the thought of it with him into his solitude.

When Mr Norman Angell wrote 'The Great Illusion', he argued that since the nations of Europe were economically and financially interdependent, there could not be a European war. Wherein lay his mistake? Precisely in confusing the existence of interdependence with the consciousness of it, and the consciousness of it in a form which would constitute a mutuality of experience, including an emotional and practical mutuality. It is precisely such a mistake that dogs the footsteps of all theories which identify society with the group. The group is constituted by a *de facto* interdependence, not by any consciousness thereof, not, that is to say, by society. If in a particular case the group does coincide with the limits of a social consciousness, that is a matter of accident. One of the conditions of such coincidence, as both Rousseau and the Greeks realized, is that the group should be small and compact. Another, which they did not recognize, is that the group should be relatively primitive and unselfconscious. This may be the reason why Sociology has scored its successes in the consideration of primitive types of human life, or in dealing with institutions, such as marriage, which have persisted relatively unchanged from primitive times.

In conclusion, we may note certain implications of the adjectival conception of society which have a direct bearing upon our social philosophy. All human experience is inherently social. This means, in the first place, that it involves always a reference to other persons. Thought, for instance, is not merely objective in the sense that it involves a reference to an object thought about. It involves also a reference to other persons with whom the thought is shareable. Plato was right in defining thought as a dialogue which the soul holds with itself, though it might be more accurate to say 'a conversation which the self holds with an imaginary other'. The mere fact that thought requires expression shows this, since expression is primarily communication. We may express this from another angle by saying that all our experience is ideally social. It is always shared in idea. This involves the thought of its actual sharing, so that it is actually incomplete until it is actually shared. Actual society is the sharing of experience, and the impulse to realize in actuality the social nature of individual experience is inherent in the experience itself. In this sense, human nature realizes itself only in society, that is to say, in the sharing of experience, not in what is commonly called 'group life'. We should notice also in this connection that the development of individual experience with its potentiality of society involves right at its origin some realization of actual society. Speech itself is a sharing of experience; and if we did not realize in fact the mutuality of this shared experience we could never learn to speak.

Solitary experience, then, is experience which is imperfectly realized, which is baulked and frustrated in the realization of its own nature. Human experience is fully real only in the sharing of experience between individuals.

What, then, is the relation between society in this sense and the formation of groups? What, for instance, is the relation between society and the State? Obviously, on this conception of society, the State is not society, for it would be absurd to suggest that there was any real sharing of experience between all the individuals who comprise the State. On the other hand, States do facilitate the sharing of experience in a thousand ways. The State, like any group, is a mechanism, an organization for the facilitation of society. To say that the State exists to further the welfare of society is, on this view, mere nonsense. For it implies that society is an entity. But the State, or any organization which links individuals together, exists to make society possible, to provide a mechanism through which the sharing of human experience may be achieved in a progressively fuller measure. In this connection, we must carefully rule out a preconception which comes from the substantial view of society. A State is a territorial unit; and its function is to facilitate human intercourse within the territory which it governs. This is not the same thing as to say that its business is to facilitate intercourse between its own citizens. That is a mere limitation *ab extra*. It is just as much the function of the State to further the sharing of experience between foreigners who meet within its territory. Society has no inherent reference to citizenship or nationality.

Further, on this view, a 'group' like the State is merely a mechanism, and therefore a means to an end, and its value is an economic value. It has no value in itself. There is nothing sacrosanct or inherently valuable about it. It is a complex of institutions for the furtherance of society, not itself society. If therefore it proves to be a hindrance rather than a furtherance of society, if it tends to block or limit the sharing of human experience, it loses its value and needs to be replaced as a good workman replaces an unserviceable tool. The State has no rights, no authority, for it is an instrument, not an agent; a network of organization, not a person. Such authority as State officials rightfully exercise is derivative from the function which the State fulfils in the furtherance and facilitation of society between individuals. Lastly, this adjectival conception of society gives a new meaning to the familiar view that all morality, all duties and obligations, all right and all rights are social. For in insisting on this it does not mean that they depend in any sense upon the existence of determinate groups of people, living in interdependence. The only logical issue of such a view, and it is the common view, is Hobbism. It means rather that it is from the social reference, the mutuality, of individual human experience that all value takes its origin. The social character of human nature is the full expression of its objectivity. To say that all human experience is social and to say that it is ideally objective or rational means in the long run the same thing. And the reality of goodness, of right, of obligation depends upon objectivity.

Seven

Government by
the People

In the historical process by which our knowledge develops, new ideas and new experiences tend very naturally to define themselves by reference to the old. It is not merely that an original thinker must express his originality in terms of old modes of language and thought (which is true and important), but that the new idea, the new experience, being vague and indistinctly grasped, is apt to coin for its expression and propagation phrases in which the emphasis falls upon the difference or variation from what is familiar and concretely understood. In the history of practical developments like that of the theory of political organization this factor is both evident and momentous. In the transition to modern democracy, for example, the familiar distinction between the Sovereign and Subjects dictates the form in which the old order is challenged. The 'People' takes up arms against the 'King'. The Will of the People challenges the Will of the Prince. The establishment of democratic institutions is conceived as the transference of Sovereignty to the People, and government by the People takes the place of government by the Monarch. Such a progress of thought is inevitable, and indeed essential, in the early stages of the struggle for freedom. It is enough to be clear what one is fighting against, and to adopt as the war-cry a phrase which is inspired by the negation of the hated tyranny, and of its familiar claims to right. But as time passes, when freedom has been gained and its institutions have become the familiar institutions; when the old

---

[1] From 'Government by the People', *Journal of Philosophical Studies*, 2 (1927), pp. 532–43.

order has in its turn grown vague and half-mythical, the democratic war-cry persists as a positive definition of the new political
organization. Then it becomes in its inaccuracy a positive danger,
the weapon of obscurantism and reaction, and no longer of the
effort to achieve and understand. So long as government by the
monarch was a brutal fact or a passionate memory the slogan
'Government by the People' had a powerful pragmatic value in its
negation of the yoke that was burdening men's shoulders and blis-
tering their minds. Now that the old oppression is no more, and
that the phrase has gained the status of a hallowed expression of
our positive liberties, its ancient value has been transformed into a
blinkering superstition, which serves rather to keep the monarchical idea galvanized than to further the process of its dissolution.

No modern state ever did, ever could, or ever desired to govern
itself. When we recur to the historical movements which ushered
in the modern political world, we discover at once how palpably
inadequate these phrases are to describe what was really happening. The king was not at war with the people. In England's Civil
War the struggle was between two parties, divided not by position or wealth, but by a common attitude in regard to the religious
and the economic questions of the day, and in it half the people at
least were indifferent to the issues at stake. In France the revolution was indeed a class war, but a class war brought about not by a
desire of the people for self-government, but as a rising of the
oppressed classes against a government envisaging a national
glory and developing a national policy which was both vastly
expensive and blindly indifferent to the welfare of the masses of
its subjects. In neither case was the execution of the king the occasion of a popular shout of triumph, but of a revulsion of feeling.
This at least was not what the People had fought to achieve. The
People indeed was no single unit opposed to its rulers, and claim-
ing the rights which custom, law and theory ascribed to the sovereign, but a mass of suffering thwarted human beings, with the
most varied interests and purposes, united to demand that their
feelings and their needs should be taken into account, that they
should be free from vexations in their private lives, especially that
they should not be taxed to maintain a national ambition which
they did not share, and to support a national power from which
they reaped no benefit; a people bewildered and misled by

quacks and agitators, struggling often against their own conscience and its sense of loyalty to law and authority, or a party
whose leaders demanded a free field for personal initiative in religion and in commerce. In a word, the democrats fought, not for
government by the people, not for the transference of political
authority to their own shoulders, but for the modification of obso-
lete conceptions of authority, for the limitations of arbitrary
power, for some freedom of initiative for private individuals in
the building up of complex national life. They found that to
achieve their purpose they must limit the field of political activity,
that to limit this authority they must make government responsible, and that to make government responsible they must make it
representative.

Unfortunately, by the time that experience of the practical
development of democratic institutions had been gained sufficient to make a positive reconstruction of theory possible, the
realistic rationalism of Hobbes and the experimental rationalism
of Locke had given way to the Romantic Idealism of Rousseau.
The French revolution, long overdue and spectacular in its bitter-
ness and violence, struck the imagination of Europe in the early
days of the Romantic movement. Romanticism was in no mind to
bow itself to the Baal of fact. With all the fervour of his imagination and his unbalanced temperament Rousseau seized upon the
negative revolutionary slogan 'Government by the Will of the
People', and transformed it into the positive metaphysical
hypothesis of the Sovereignty of the 'General Will'. The new and
vital conception of the organic nature of social life was thus translated into terms of the old monarchical institutions by a personifi-
cation of the 'People'; and in popular thought the idea of
democracy as self-government was perpetuated and sanctified.
The Romantic tradition in philosophy, following the lead of Rousseau, proceeded for more than a century to develop this theoretical formulation of the living unity of the democratic state,
discarding the cruder elements of the Rousseau theory, adapting
it to the representative character of modern political life, and
growing more and more subtle in its effort to digest or to dispose
of the palpable difficulties. Bosanquet's great work, *The Philosophical Theory of the State*, is the perfect achievement of this ingenious
and misguided effort. It opens with a discussion of the 'paradox

of self-government', and continues with elaborate erudition and ingenuity, as well as with a sincere and worthy idealism, to resolve the paradox. Yet the more complete the success of the attempt grows, the more remote does the conclusion seem from the practical problems of actual political life, until it forces a passionate protest against metaphysics and metaphysicians from the bewildered reader, or a regretful sigh that unfortunately what is all right in theory would never do in practice. The fact is that the paradox of self-government is no true paradox, but simply a contradiction, and that all this ingenuity, considered as an effort to understand the nature and movement of modern democratic states, is so much wasted effort. More than this, by supplying a theory which supports and maintains a more popular conception of democracy which has remained traditional, but which has less and less obvious bearings upon our political problems, it perverts, if we accept it, our understanding of these, and our efforts towards political reform, or if we are compelled by the logic of facts to reject or disregard it, leaves us at the mercy of a blind opportunism.

Such an indictment of the philosophical theory of the Sovereignty of the General Will, and of its popular embodiment in the conception of democracy as Government by the People, requires careful substantiation. It is no valid ground for attack, to complain that the theory is idealistic and incapable of immediate application to political practice in our world of half-lights and semi-selfishness. For in this sense any political theory is necessarily the presentation of an ideal, an effort to understand the real nature of democracy, or to speak more frankly, an attempt to define not what the modern state in fact is, but what it is seeking to be, to estimate the direction of the democratic movement by envisaging its goal, and so to provide a standard by which to guide ourselves in our efforts to improve the political machinery still further. Our quarrel with the theory of 'Government by the People' is that it defines, not the ideal of the democratic movement, but something entirely different; and that the movements of confessedly democratic reform have brought us, not nearer to the realization of the Sovereignty of the General Will, but further away from it in a progress towards a goal which is in some senses almost its opposite. It is of this conviction that a justification must be offered.

Two of the most noteworthy features of Rousseau's political doctrine are his repudiation of representative institutions and his opposition to religious autonomy. Legislation through a Representative Assembly, he stoutly maintains, is incompatible with political freedom and with popular sovereignty. In the church and in the particular religious loyalties which it sets up he sees a pregnant instance of the greatest danger against which free government has to guard with unceasing vigilance, the danger of particular interests within the state, whether of individuals or of groups, setting up their wills against the paramount will of the people. Yet the development of representative institutions and the withdrawal of the religious aspect of life from state-interference are precisely the hall-marks of democratic achievement. The long struggles for religious freedom were the birth-throes of democracy. State interference in the proper field of religion is the denial of the very roots of democracy, and representative institutions are the main characteristic and the basic safeguard of any democratic organization. Surely a theory of the state which offers as the ideal of democracy an organization which excludes representative legislation and a temper which would make the state paramount in the religious field is self-condemned.

It will be replied, no doubt, that Rousseau was mistaken in considering that his general theory dictated such conclusions, and that room has been found within the framework of the Sovereignty of the Will of the People both for religious toleration and for representative institutions. No doubt this is true. Undoubtedly modern theorists of the Rousseau tradition, and modern popular conceptions with them, have adapted, often with convincing ingenuity, the doctrine of the Sovereignty of the General will to these modern demands. But even if Rousseau was wrong in his contention, it is strange and disturbing to find a theory of the modern state having to use subtlety to accommodate, as if they were side-shows of the exhibition, what are without doubt the essential features in the evolution of modern democracy. In our general thought, at least, the accommodation is far from satisfactory. It makes room for both political and religious authority in the same world by refusing to take either very seriously, and by refraining from pushing the issue to any conclusion. It 'accommodates' representative legislation by conceiving it as somehow a second-best forced upon us by the exigencies of the modern situation, particularly by the size and complexity of the nation-state. Parliament is thus represented as a miniature of the nation, in which all shades of opinion ought to be reflected, as in a mirror, so that it may do for the people what the people has a right to do for itself, what the people would do for itself, were it not too large and too complex a body. Such an attitude, by blurring the distinction between the function of the electorate and the function of the legislative assembly, which are complementary, and by assigning to Parliament by delegation the whole legislative authority of the people, works out as a defence of Parliamentary Absolutism, and leads straight to the absurd conclusion that Parliament has the right to pass any law that it pleases. The more philosophical theory, with a more general grasp of the theoretical demands of such a claim, seeks to find a moral basis for the supposed obligation on the individual to accept the absolute authority of the Sovereign People, and so far as it succeeds, becomes in practice the defender of state absolutism on a moral basis.

Is it, however, so certain that Rousseau was mistaken in thinking that the sovereignty of the Popular Will was incompatible with religious autonomy, and with representative government? Consider the problem which he set himself to solve. 'The problem is', he says, 'to find a form of association which will defend and protect, with the whole common force, the person and goods of each associate, and in which each, while uniting himself with all, may still obey himself alone, and remain as free as before' (*The Social Contract*, I. Vi). With this formulation I have in general no fault to find. It goes to the root of the matter, and states the fundamental demand of free government. 'Why', we may ask, 'the stringent insistence that a man should "obey himself alone"?' The answer, as the subsequent development of the theory clearly shows, is that the moral nature of man makes him ineluctably responsible for his actions. No man *can* sell himself into slavery. He cannot shift his moral responsibility on to the shoulders of another. How then can this responsibility, which is necessarily personal, be reconciled with an obligation to obey a law? How can a man retain the free initiative which is alone compatible with moral responsibility, and yet have his conduct dictated by an authority external to him?

As Rousseau sees, if the authority imposing the obligation is really external to him, no solution is possible. A law which is to be a moral obligation must be imposed by the agent upon himself. This can hardly be disputed; and therefore it would seem that the only line along which a solution can be sought is one which identifies the individual, as a moral agent, with the community to which he belongs. This line of solution is no new one. Plato had explored it already with great thoroughness. To act morally is to act not with reference to any private good, but with reference to the general good. Moral obligation is essentially social obligation. The moral will of the individual is therefore a general will, a will for the general good. What the general good is can only be defined socially, and the law of the community is, so far as it is true law, the definition of this good. Thus the content of the individual's moral obligation is defined for him, and can only be defined for him, by the legal structure of the society of which he forms a part. Logically, therefore, a man can only be free in obeying the law if the law furnishes him with a definition of his social duty for which he can accept responsibility as a free moral agent. If he cannot, the law ceases to be binding upon him. It cannot be binding upon him until he so accepts it. He must impose it upon himself. Under a system which involves representative legislation, however, he is denied the right to do this. He can only choose his representative, if even that. The laws enacted by the legislative assembly are supposed to bind him without any decision of his as to the moral rightness of the obligations which they impose. They are laws and binding upon him *because* they are the results of the deliberation of the legislative assembly, not because they are freely imposed by him upon himself. The responsibility for the decision of what is right rests upon the representatives, not upon the subjects. And this the very nature of moral obligation must deny. A man may seek help in deciding what his duty is, but the ultimate decision must lie with himself if he is to bear the responsibility for his action. It would seem then that Rousseau is right in holding that his solution of the problem of freedom in society is incompatible with representative institutions.

What, in general terms, is that solution? Freed from the terminology of the social contract, and restated in the way that Rousseau's followers in modern times have restated it, the solution is as follows. Moral obligation is essentially a social thing. Formally, it is the obligation upon every individual to will the good, and to realize the good. But when we ask what the good is, we discover that it is not the good of this individual or of that group of associated individuals, but a good which includes all lesser goods, organizing them systematically in their due relations to one another in terms of a universal purpose. The moral end is an end which takes up into itself all lesser and particular ends, a purpose which includes all lesser purposes and allows them to function within it as contributions to the greater purpose which is the good of the whole. This whole is the community, which is the real unit of human life. The State is thus the real moral organism in which each one of us is a functional member. Our duties are only to be determined in relation to the greater whole in which we have our due place and function. Our obligation is to realize the inclusive and harmonious good of the community of which we are members. Only by individual action can it be realized. But what that inclusive good is can only be determined by the structure of the whole community, embodied in its institutions and laws. Under ideal conditions, therefore, the laws and institutions of the state would define for each individual his moral duty because they would be the concrete embodiment of a common purpose in which his own purpose was included, and given a moral because a universal and social meaning. So, there could be no conflict between the moral responsibility of the individual and the obligations imposed by the law of the state. So, the general will would have become actual, and government by the people would have been realized.

It is not my purpose to embark upon a philosophical refutation of this position. It seems to me to be, in fact, fundamentally unsound, in that it overlooks the simple, but important point that the state is a territorial unit, and seeks to base the validity of law not on its being law, but on its being morally right. What I do wish to indicate is that this is not the ideal towards which the development of modern democracy has been working, that in fact every forward stride in democratic organization takes us farther away from this conception. If it is the true ideal of the state, then the modern world has been moving for the last three hundred years in a completely wrong direction. So far from attempting to make the state an inclusive moral organism, taking up into its universal purpose all lesser purposes and interests, we have fought to rescue from state-control the whole of the cultural and moral activities of life. Freedom of conscience, freedom of association, freedom of individual initiative, freedom for any man who wills to plan creatively and accomplish his purpose, freedom for small minorities from the tyranny, not only of government officials, but of public opinion — these are the things for which democracy has striven and still is striving. We have aimed, and surely rightly, to prevent the complex of organic institutions, whether acting through the unformulated pressure of custom and convention or through the organized mechanism of political authority, from throttling the liberty and power of individual human beings to live spontaneously up to the limits of their capacity. For this reason we realize that the true test of the development of any nation lies in its treatment of minorities and its dealings with conscientious objectors, and we have grave doubts of any government which uses its educational institutions to inculcate any particular type of culture.

When we look at the concrete history of modern states, we see without difficulty that it is the story of a progressive effort to limit the field, while increasing the effectiveness, of political authority. It was no attempt to transfer to the people in its collective capacity the omnicompetent sovereignty once claimed by monarchs. Now, from the very dawn of political history the instrument for the control of government has been law. It is in our attitude to law, perhaps, that we may find the root cause of most of the muddle-headedness of our political theories. We have a peculiar tendency to think of law as if it were merely a criminal code, and to think of a criminal code in terms of the Old Testament decalogue. As a result we imagine that law is a formulation and imposition of duties upon its subjects by some sovereign authority. When thereafter we wish to justify law, we seek to show that the duties which it imposes are morally valid, and therefore binding upon the consciences of men. Yet if we stop to think, we may find it surprising that laws have normally, in European history at least, been extorted from the authorities by a rebellious people, rendered restive or even savage by misrule. The main effect of the defining of a law is to define and so to restrict the authority which must carry the law into execution. If law then is a command at all, it is a command to the government. It issues instructions to an executive which define the limitations within which they may exercise the power entrusted to them. This is in itself a great step in the direction of individual freedom. So long, however, as the executive officers are also legislative and judicial officers, it is difficult to make this check effective. The great step forward which is taken by democracy consists in making the executive responsible to an elected legislative assembly. The executive then cannot make the laws which it administers, and so secure to itself whatever powers it needs for carrying out its purposes. Government still remains government by executive officials, but these officials have no powers but such as are conferred upon them by law, which is their charter of rights.

But this, it may be said, simply results in making Parliament sovereign, and the executive authority its servant; and since Parliament is elected by the people and so controlled by the people, it is the people which is sovereign in the last resort, and government is by the people after all. This is altogether too simple-minded. For in the first place the function of Parliament is limited to the modification of the existing law through a very complicated system of procedure, and in the second place the people has not the right to legislate. We must consider these two points separately.

The legislative function of Parliament is exercised against a background of existing law. This existing law is a very complex and highly organized system of great power. Its interpretation is in the hands of a judiciary which is all but completely independent both of the legislative and of the executive. With the processes of the administration and interpretation of this law neither the executive nor the legislative may interfere. The judge may not appeal to Parliament even when he is in difficulties as to the precise meaning of a recent statute, nor may Parliament instruct him of its own accord. To this law the private citizen may appeal against any illegal use of power by an executive official, and if he can prove his case, the executive must bow to the decision of the court. A Parliamentary statute, when interpreted by the courts in terms of the rules of legal procedure and legal precedent, when worked into the organic system of existing law, sometimes is found to work in practice in a way which was obviously not intended by Parliament. In that case, Parliament must either grin and bear it, or go to the very considerable trouble of making another statute to take its place.

This modification of the existing law by the formulation of new legal instruments, which is the function of a legislative assembly, is itself a complex procedure governed by strict rules. A statute is made, not merely by a certain body, or rather by certain bodies of persons, but in a prescribed fashion, and the manner of its making is more important than the persons who are concerned in its manufacture. The way of a bill, even if it be the bill of a government with a large Parliamentary majority, is beset with pitfalls. It must run the gauntlet of a well-informed and active criticism, sensitive to public opinion, for which the prizes of success are the fruits of office. The power of a government to carry its purposes into law are severely limited, not merely by the voting strength of the opposition, but much more by the debating power of the opposition, and by the quality of the votes which it can itself command. There is a point beyond which an increase in the government majority in Parliament is a source of weakness and not of strength. A large number of supporters elected by narrow majorities in the constituencies paralyses a government's freedom of action, and acts as a most effective brake upon partisan legislation. In these and many other ways the power of Parliament, even as a legislative assembly, is severely controlled. To talk of the British Parliament having the right to pass any law it pleases is palpably absurd. One might as well inform a working miner with a large family, during a slump in trade, that if he does not like the conditions in the industry in which he is engaged, he is entirely free to find another occupation.

Parliament, however, is ultimately responsible to the electorate and its authority is a derivative authority. Is then the people sovereign? Is government for this reason government by the people? By no means. If the function of Parliament itself is not government, but the modification under strict rules of procedure of the existing legal system, the function of the people, as an electorate, is the control of Parliament. This control is itself a special and limited function. The electorate has not the right to initiate legislation. It cannot pass or veto any law. When the electorate turns out a government, its action has no effect upon the validity of the laws made under the auspices of that government. How then does it control government? The answer is simple and straightforward. The electorate controls Parliament by its choice of representatives. This in effect gives to the people the right and the power to determine policy in legislation. Policy is a vague term, but there are certain elements in its connotation which can be defined. It involves the determination of the problems which shall be the subject of legislation and therefore of executive action, and it determines the order of their relative importance. It involves further the determination of the general temper in which a solution of these problems shall be sought. One has only to look at the effects of any extension of the franchise to see that its immediate effect is to bring a new range of issues prominently before the attention of the legislative body, and to alter the general tone of their discussion. The main object is not to give to the people the right to make the laws which they must obey. It is not of supreme importance that an elector should be sufficiently educated to have a definite opinion about the worth or effectiveness of certain legislative proposals. It is essential that he should have a chance to say, 'Here and here the existing social system is irking and baffling me and my fellows. This and that are the problems which must be solved by state action'. It is also necessary that he should be able to choose as a member of the legislative assembly someone who understands his difficulties and sympathizes with them. And these two things are quite independent of any ability to determine the line which the legislative solution should take. *That*, after all, can only be determined by a painstaking and scientific investigation of facts and conditions, and by a careful forecast of the practical effects of suggested solutions. It is essential to good government that the people should not dictate the laws to the legislative assembly. Broadly, then, we may conclude that on the institutional side, through the development of representative institutions, democracy has secured, not government by the people, but the control of an expert government; and that this control has been secured by granting to the electorate the power to determine policy, while reserving for a special assembly the right, within the restrictions of a defined procedure, to modify and extend the existing system of law.

Such a point of view does justice to the place held in the development of the modern state by representative institutions. But there is more behind. The reason for subjecting government to control was in the first instance the need for securing the liberty of the individual conscience, particularly in matters of religion. To assert against government the right of the individual to worship God in his own way, without let or hindrance, was to refuse to admit the sovereignty of the state in the field of religion. At first sight this might seem a small concession. But it is of the essence of religion to control the whole life of culture and conscience, to unify and to inspire it. To drive the state from the religious field means in the long run to drive it from the whole cultural field, and so to insist upon the autonomy of culture and upon the autonomy of the individual in all matters of conscience. Behind the democratic movement lies the Christian insistence upon the supreme and final value of individual personality. Rousseau was right in thinking that the claims of the Churches were directed against the conception of the state as a moral person, and involved an attack upon this theory of the general will. The demand of the reformers was from the first, implicitly, that the state should cease to regard itself as the focus of the nation's cultural life, and supreme over individual moral purposes. The reformers were successful. As democracy has developed, the state has become less and less concerned with moral and cultural issues, more and more confined to a field which is concerned with contracts and damages, or with the provision of the material support within which an autonomous culture can live and develop. Laws resting on moral and cultural grounds have disappeared from the statute-book or fallen into disuse; while laws dealing with the material organization of life have developed apace. It is no longer really possible to conceive law as the definition or imposition of a moral rule. It is rather the plan of co-operation within an intricate society of individuals. The state has been driven from the moral field, and restricted to a limited field; it is no longer an inclusive unity of a personal kind, but an abstract aspect of the social life. Its territorial limitations, its externality, though they may form the necessary basis of any social culture, are too narrow and too material to bind and determine a moral and spiritual outlook which becomes daily more international and universal, more inward and creative.

In this there is revealed a different answer to Rousseau's fundamental problem. There is a wide aspect of social life, which demands increasing organization of an authoritative kind, but which raises no issues which can be matters of conscience. It is essential that there should be a rule of the road, but it cannot be a matter of conscience that it should be one rule rather than another. Suppose that the authority of government could be limited to this large and growing field. Then there could be no clash between the conscience of the individual and the obligations imposed by law, and the moral agent could 'remain as free as before, obeying himself alone'. And though this ideal also remains still remote from our actual achievement, it yet would seem to be the goal towards which the modern state has slowly but surely been groping its way. Equally it is the antithesis of the ideal which is enshrined in our general conception of 'Government by the People'.

Does this ideal reduce the state to a bare expediency? Only if we forget that the state has its essential place in the wider and higher life of moral responsibility. Political obligation is a derivative obligation, but it is derivative from the moral obligation of the individual, and therefore carries with it the categorical character of all moral duty. As individual persons in an organic social network we have a binding duty to act justly in all our relations with our fellows. But in the complicated societies in which we live this obligation can only be fulfilled through the maintenance and development of a system of law, and of an executive authority to administer the law. The basis of the state is the categorical imperative of justice. Yet even in the moral life justice is no all-inclusive obligation, but merely its basis and its beginning.

Eight

Freedom in the Personal Nexus

The traditional formulations of the problem of human freedom are so abstract that they have neither substance nor meaning. Or perhaps it would be more appropriate to say that they have substance and meaning only as it is lent to them by the personal interests and assumptions of individuals, so that they change from generation to generation, from country to country, from circumstance to circumstance. If the issue is to be put in the way of solution we must begin by determining what we are discussing when we discuss freedom. This cannot be done by any mere definition of terms, which would carry no further than the use of the word in the present context. We must determine the locus of the problem in universal human experience. We must discover the centre of disturbance. We must put our finger upon the concrete origin of the question, if it is to be real and not artificial; a problem of life and not of language.

The traditional dilemma of free will or determinism is entirely artificial, like most exclusive alternatives of a high order of abstraction. If a rigid determinism obtained in the field of human behaviour there could, of course, be no choice; and equally if a rigid freedom of will prevailed there could be no choice either, since both alternatives would be equally open. But it would be a waste of energy to pursue an abstract argument when it is easy to see by inspection that the debate is artificial. We need only suppose that we have accepted either alternative, and ask what dif-

[1]   From 'Freedom in the Personal Nexus', in *Freedom: Its Meaning*, ed. Ruth N. Anshen (New York: Harcourt, 1940; London: Allen and Unwin, 1942), pp. 176–93.

ference it makes in concrete experience. If everything is determined, it still remains unquestionably that a man is freer out of prison than in it; freer in America at peace than in Germany at war; freer in health than in sickness, freer when he has money in his pocket than when he is penniless. If man possesses freedom of will equally these variations in freedom remain unaffected. The locus of the real problem lies in these variations of human freedom under varying conditions. The question is not, 'Are we free?' but 'How free are we?.' It is not, 'Have we freedom of will?' but 'Under what conditions have we most freedom of will?'.

Men have craved freedom, demanded freedom, and fought for freedom. This proves that they have meant by 'freedom' something that could be achieved by human effort; and not something that we either have or lack. If the free-will controversy were more than a scholastic wrangle, nothing could be done about freedom, whichever of the two alternatives were correct. This fact throws a curious light upon the metaphysical controversy itself. If we can increase freedom by taking the appropriate action, then freedom must be conditioned. It is only by altering its conditions that we can increase or diminish freedom. We can diminish a man's freedom of action by locking him in a room, and so changing the conditions of his action. To say that anything is conditioned is to say that it is determined. The conditions are its determinants. Thus what men have always meant by freedom, is itself determined. In theory they have assumed that if everything is determined there can be no freedom. Yet what if freedom itself is determined? We tend to think too easily that men long for freedom that is denied them by the forces of nature and history. Perhaps the opposite is nearer to the truth. Perhaps man is only too anxious to escape from a freedom which nature and history combine to thrust upon his timidity. Perhaps we are destined to be free whether we like it or not. To be free is to be responsible. To evade responsibility is to flee from freedom. If it is true that the inexorable laws of human development compel man to accept an ever increasing responsibility for his own destiny, then freedom is determined at the metaphysical level, as an inevitable product of the laws of nature. In that event freedom and determinism are implicates, not contradictories.

There is also a subjective factor in the problem which demands preliminary attention. No one, I imagine, would consider that we are not free because there are many things that we are unable to do. A drowning determinist, clutching at straws, would hardly contend that we are not free because we cannot pay weekend visits to the moon. Freedom has clearly some relation to our desires, and our desires have their roots in the same nature of things that determine the possibilities of our action. No man can intend to do what he knows or believes to be beyond the bounds of possibility. It is doubtful whether we can even seriously desire, for any length of time, what we believe to be unobtainable. Freedom seems to lie in some *ratio* between our desires and our capacity to satisfy them; between what we can intend and what we can achieve. At least we may satisfy ourselves that men experience the lack of freedom only when their efforts are frustrated; only when they fail to achieve what they believe to be possible. The social function of the agitator, which has sometimes been of high importance in the history of freedom, is to persuade men to envisage, to desire, and to demand a freedom that they do not possess. His difficulty often lies in convincing the people that they are in bondage. His success depends upon convincing them that the new forms of life he proposes are really possible. The contented man is free, as the sages have always told us, because his powers are adequate to his desires. They have, perhaps, been too ready to assume that any man can be contented if he chooses. Even if he could, it is not at all clear that he ought to be. At any rate, it is important not to overlook this subjective factor in freedom. Men's desires vary. Their conceptions of what is possible are not fixed. Consequently, what is freedom for one man may be slavery for another, and the vision of a new possibility may turn freedom into bondage.

It would appear, then, that freedom, as we experience it, resides in the adequacy to our purposes of our powers, opportunities, and means. Its opposite is the experience of constraint, which varies when for any reason we must refrain from doing what we ourselves desire to do, or must do something other than we would. But this general formulation is too wide for our purpose. It covers checks to the spontaneity of our behaviour which appear as mere momentary vexations, no sooner felt than overcome; as well as those major and permanent frustrations that may make life not worth living. We have, as it were, drawn a circle round the field within which the problem is to be located. We must try to discover its centre. We have included all cases; we have to determine which are the crucial cases. The answer which I wish to suggest is that the centre of the problem of freedom lies in the nexus of personal relationships, and that all other types of constraint are derivative from the constraints of personal relationship, at least if they are real.

Before explaining this view, it will be well to consider the distinction between real and illusory freedom which I have introduced as qualification. There is, we have seen, a subjective element in freedom, and it is, of course, on this account that freedom can be illusory. But the distinction between 'subjective' and 'objective' must be used in this context with extreme care. The ordinary distinction between the two is derived from the reflective field, in which we 'stand over against' the world, in contemplation or in thought. In this attitude, whatever we consider is independent of the processes of consideration. It is 'objective' in the sense that our activities of observing and thinking 'make no difference' to it. But freedom is not objective in this sense; neither is it a property or character of anything objective. Freedom is a modality of action, and actions are not contemplated but performed. Here indeed lies the formal defect of the question, 'Is the will free?'. It postulates an objective entity called 'the will', and inquires whether it possesses an objective property called 'freedom'. The phrase 'my will' stands for 'me acting', in contrast to 'me observing and reflecting'. Acting means realizing an intention, and an act cannot therefore be merely objective. Neither can it be merely subjective. It is a unit of experience which begins in the 'subjective' and terminates in the 'objective'. It bridges the gap between 'mind' and 'matter', between the 'self' and the 'world', between 'ideas' and 'things', if indeed there is any gap to be bridged. Freedom, as a modality of this transition from subjective to objective, cannot be either merely subjective or merely objective. We must guard against the tendency to identify the illusory with the subjective and the real with the objective in this context. All freedom has both a subjective and an objective element in it, and these are not separable. They are rather aspects of one and the same thing. We are not necessarily free merely because we feel free; but on the other hand a constraint which is not felt is no real constraint. A contented slave is still a slave, though his slavery is bondage for him; and when the poet writes that

> Stone walls do not a prison make,
> Nor iron bars a cage

we understand what he means, but refuse to take his statement *au pied de la lettre*. If freedom is to be real it must not be subject to destruction by a change of mood or an increase in knowledge. It must be rooted, as a subjective experience, in the objective nature of things. Otherwise it is illusory.

We may distinguish two types of illusory freedom, which we may call subjective and objective respectively. Freedom, we may say, is subjectively illusory, if the absence of any experience of constraint depends upon the absence of a desire to do what one would be prevented from doing. It is objectively illusory if the feeling of freedom depends upon a false belief in our power to achieve what we desire. The stoic ideal of a freedom to be achieved by getting rid of desire and 'willing what happens' is the apotheosis of subjectively illusory freedom. Kant's effort to equate freedom with moral obligation falls into the same category. Desires which are suppressed do not cease to exist; they are at best inactive in consciousness. The objective type of illusory freedom is even more common. It exists wherever we overestimate our capacities or our means; or are ignorant of the obstacles in circumstances to the achievement of our intentions. Corresponding to these illusory freedoms, there are illusory constraints. We are subject to illusions of weakness as well as of power; and we are afflicted with spurious desires, which lead us to demand impossible satisfactions that we do not really want, and which, if we were to achieve them, we should repudiate. The illusory character of such freedoms and constraints does not consist in their non-existence or their ineffectiveness. We are not dealing with ideas which have no counterpart in the real world. In action the subjective does not confront the objective as it does in reflection. Action passes *from* the subjective *to* the objective. It is a process in time, with an inherent reference to the future. The check to action which destroys our freedom in action may come at any point in the process. Illusory freedom is experienced as freedom. But it is incompatible with its own persistence, and is therefore self-defeating. We are not free to achieve the impossible. But we are often free *in* actions which must inevitably lead to frustration, because their objective, unknown to us, is in fact impossible. Such freedom is properly called illusory, since it depends upon illusions, and must lead to its own destruction.

With this distinction between real and illusory freedom in mind, we may return to the central issue. Real freedom depends upon the character of the nexus of personal relations in which we are involved. This is the thesis which I wish to expound. It can be expressed and understood best by drawing attention to the kind of experience of freedom and constraint which it makes the centre of the problem. If I am in the company of strangers whose good will is important to me, and cannot be depended on, my conversation with them and my behaviour towards them suffer from constraint. I cannot express myself spontaneously. I must think carefully before I speak, and seek to make a good impression. I must act a part; I cannot 'be myself'. If I leave this company and join a number of intimate friends whom I know and trust, this constraint disappears and is replaced by freedom. I can now allow my whole self to appear. I can say what comes in to my mind. I can behave 'naturally'. I need not fear criticism, and so I can be spontaneous, speaking and acting without an eye upon effects. Here then is one familiar type of experience in which the contrast between 'freedom' and 'constraint' appears. My thesis is that this contrast is the central one; and that when we wish to go to the root of the problem of freedom, this is precisely the sort of case which we should accept as a type instance, and have in mind as an example. My reason for saying this is not that there are no other types of cases which are important, such as those which form the stock-in-trade of all discussions of political liberty. It is that the type of experience I have chosen involves, in principle, all the others; that if it is understood, then all the others are, in principle, understood; if it is solved, then all the others are soluble. The understanding of other types, on the other hand, is not possible, or at least cannot be complete, unless this type of case is understood; nor can the problem be solved in the other types of instances unless it is solved in this type. I believe, in other words, that the problem of freedom appears at different levels of experience, and that its solution at the upper levels depends upon its solution on the basic level. And I believe that if we consider the problem as it appears in the nexus of direct personal relationships, we are attacking it at ground level; we are laying bare its foundations. Only if we do this is it possible to envisage a radical solution. Even if such a radical solution is impracticable, it will still enable us to understand what partial solutions are possible and practicable at other levels, such as the political or the economic; and it will prevent us from expecting too much from reforms that do not go to the root of the trouble.

In our effort to determine the general field in which the real problem of freedom arises, we noticed that it was not the mere absence of power that created the problem, but the absence of power relative to a real desire. We noticed further that a real desire — the kind of desire that can give rise to deliberate action — depends upon a belief in the possibility of its satisfaction. This involved a curious paradox. It would seem that we can only experience a real loss of freedom in the presence of an impossible possibility. I do not mean by this that we must believe something to be possible which is in fact impossible; for this is the situation in which we enjoy a freedom which is objectively illusory. We must find ourselves in a situation in which a real possibility is actually impossible to realize; in which we believe, and believe rightly, that what we desire to achieve can be achieved and at the same time cannot be achieved. For it is only in such conditions that we can experience a real frustration of our will. It is only then that we feel, and rightly feel, that we are *prevented* from realizing our intentions, that we are *deprived* of our freedom.

How can such a situation arise? Surely any action that I propose is either possible or impossible. At most, it would seem, I may be mistaken in thinking it possible when it is impossible, or impossible when it is not. Surely it cannot both *be* possible and impossible at the same time. Logically, of course, it cannot. But logic does not have the last word.

For our logical judgments depend upon the distinction between subjective and objective, which holds in the field of reflection but not in the field of action. In reflection about the nature of the objective world we are guided by the postulate that all unreason falls into the subjective field; so that if any illogicality comes to light it must belong to the processes of thinking, and not to what is the object of our thought. But in action the unreason of the subjective field is carried over into the objective, and our mistakes are objectively revealed and have an objective embodiment. If two of us differ in our conclusions about an objective question, then the disagreement makes no difference to the fact; it merely shows that one of us at least is mistaken, and out to change his mind. The error of another cannot here by its mere existence destroy the correctness of my own judgment. His inability to think logically does not interfere with the freedom of my own processes of thought. But when we pass from the sphere of thought to that of action this immunity is left behind. For in action the irrationality of others can frustrate the rationality of my intentions, and my irrationality can frustrate theirs. If our intentions contradict one another, they destroy each other's possibility. What is objectively possible becomes actually impossible. Wherever, indeed, the achievement of an intention depends upon co-operation, the simplest of objective possibilities may be made impossible by the unwillingness of those concerned to co-operate; and this unwillingness may, on occasion, rest upon completely irrational and totally absurd grounds. The capacity of human beings to 'cut off their noses to spite their faces' is very high, and it is not unusual to find a group of individuals who refuse to co-operate in the achievement of an objective which all of them desire, for reasons so irrational that they must conceal them even from themselves. This is the resolution of the paradox of the impossible possibility which lies at the root of the problem of freedom. It is the nexus of personal relationship that is responsible for the variation in human freedom. We can prevent one another from achieving our purposes, even when they are objectively possible, and so limit or destroy one another's freedom. Moreover, this is the only way in which real freedom can be limited; for only thus can what is objectively possible be rendered actually impossible. Only persons can limit the freedom of persons. Any limitation of freedom must have its source in us; in the character of our relationships, as personal agents, to one another.

It is the instinctive recognition of this truth that links the experience of a lack of freedom with the idea of oppression and tyranny. When men feel the loss of freedom they behave as though someone were responsible. They instinctively feel that some individual or class is wrongfully depriving them of a freedom which is theirs by natural right. The struggle for freedom is always a struggle against oppression. The oppressors have defended themselves on the plea that the freedom demanded was in the nature of things impossible; that the constraint complained of was in fact illusory. In this instinct there is a core of essential truth, however mistaken the accusation may be in any particular case. If men feel the loss of freedom they are always justified in looking for its source in the personal field. If men are not free, then they are oppressed. Their inability to do what they desire is not a mere lack of power, but a deprivation of power, for which the responsibility rests with their fellows. The fact that we often make mistakes in assigning the responsibility, that often indeed we are satisfied to wreak our vengeance on any available scapegoat, is no argument against this truth; any more than the fact that we often assign the wrong cause for an event suggests that it is causeless. We are therefore at liberty to lay down a principle of far-reaching importance. The solution of any problem of human freedom depends on the alteration of the relationships of persons. The importance of this principle lies in what it denies. It denies that any increase in power can solve the problem of freedom. Indeed, an increase in power which is not accompanied by a change in the nexus of personal relationships must inevitably diminish freedom. For it enlarges the field of objective possibility without altering the conditions of effective action, and so widens the gap between what can be intended and what can be achieved.

Consider two examples of this. The increase of scientific knowledge during the past century has immensely increased the range of human possibility. Much is really possible today that was objectively impossible a hundred years ago. As a result there has been a noticeable diminution of human freedom and an increase of oppression. There is nothing paradoxical about this. It is, in fact, just what must happen provided the character of the personal nexus remains, as it has remained, substantially unaltered. The increase in what is objectively possible cannot be equated with an increase in freedom. It increases the range and variety of the satisfactions that men can reasonably hope to attain. But if it leaves their forms of relationship adjusted to a narrower range of actual achievement only, then the effect is to diminish freedom. The subjective constituent of freedom must not be overlooked.

Freedom does not consist in the objective existence of power, but in the possibility of using it for desired ends. If a century of scientific development has made it possible to raise the general standard of living by 20 per cent and it has actually risen only by 10 per cent then in this respect there has been a restriction of freedom by 10 per cent. (The figures, of course, are not to be taken seriously.)

Consider, in the second place, the increase in oppression which reveals itself in modern dictatorship. In olden times a despotic monarch, however arbitrary and cruel, could interfere with the freedom of his subjects only to a quite limited extent. In a modern society with the same type of relationship between ruler and rules, the enormous increase in the range of human power involves a correspondingly enormous increase in the restriction of freedom. Not only is the tyrant's capacity to interfere with the activities of his subjects vastly increased, but the range of possible satisfactions which he can deny them is also greatly enlarged. Here again we see that an increase in objective possibility involves a decrease of freedom if the character of the personal nexus in society remains unaltered.

It might seem that this leads us to endorse the view, widely held at present, that freedom is a function of the structure of society. This is partly correct, but only partly. The more important corollary, which must be combined with this, is that the structure of society is itself a function of the personal nexus of relationship between its members. There is an ambiguity in our use of the term 'society' which is apt to result in a dangerous confusion. In general, the term refers to that nexus of relationship which binds human individuals into a unity. The ultimate fact upon which all society rests is the fact that the behaviour of each of us conditions the behaviour of the others and is therefore a determinant of their freedom. But the resulting nexus of relationship contains two distinguishable elements in virtue of the types of motive which underlie the active relationships involved. It is of the first importance to recognize, and to bear in mind, that a subjective element necessarily enters into all human behaviour, and so into the constitution of all human relationships. The elementary type forms of these contrasted motivations are hunger and love. Hunger is a motive which gives rise to actions designed to appropriate something for one's own use. Love, in contrast, is the motive of actions in which we expend what is ours upon something or someone other than ourselves. Both these types of motive are *necessary* in the sense that they belong universally to the psychological constitution of human nature and are inescapable elements in the determination of human behaviour. Both give rise to a nexus of dynamic relationships which bind us together. The first type gives rise to functional co-operation in work, and its basic forms are economic. The second gives rise to the sharing of a common life. Since the term 'society' has in our day come to be so closely bound up with discussions of the organized forms of political and economic relationship, we had better specialize it for this use, and distinguish the forms of relationship which spring from the impulse to share a common life by using the term 'community' to refer to them. The contrast to which our attention is now directed becomes thus a contrast between society and community.

The exact difference between society and community and the proper relation between them are best recognized by reference to the intentions involved. The intention involved in society lies beyond the nexus of relation which it establishes. In community it does not. It follows that society is a means to an end, while community is an end in itself. This may be stated from another angle by pointing our that a society can always be defined in terms of a common purpose, while a community cannot. Let us look, by way of example, at the simplest possible type of case, in which only two persons are involved. Two men may be associated as partners in a publishing business. They may also be associated as friends. That these two forms of relationship are different, and at least relatively independent, is shown by the fact that they may dissolve the partnership and remain friends; or they may remain in partnership and cease to be friends. Their association as partners is constituted by a co-operation in the achievement of a common purpose. Its form is dictated by this purpose. It involves a plan of co-operation and a division of labour between them. In virtue of this plan each of the two has a function in the business, in performing which he contributes his share of work to the achievement of the common purpose. Success depends on the proper co-ordination of their functions; and if the plan achieves this and each performs his function efficiently, the partnership is a satisfactory association. The whole nature of their relationship as business partners is expressible in such functional terms with reference to the common end to which the association is the means.

Now consider their relationship as friends. We are not concerned here merely with their feelings, but with the kind of active relationship which is implied in their being friends. Notice in the first place that this association cannot be defined in terms of a common purpose. We cannot ask, 'What is the purpose of their friendship?' without implying that they are not really friends, but only pretend to be friends from an ulterior motive. A relationship of this type has no purpose beyond itself. Consequently its form is not dictated by a purpose; it does not give rise of necessity to a functional division of labour. For the same reason it cannot be organized. Nevertheless it is not motiveless. Its motive is to be found in the need to share experience and to live a common life of mutual relationship, which is a fundamental constituent of human nature.

We can use the same simple instance to help us to understand the relationship of these two types of association. That they are at least partly independent of one another we have seen, since they may vary independently. But we must now notice that friendship, though it cannot be constituted by co-operation for a common purpose, necessarily generates such co-operation. A friendship which did not result in the formation of common purposes and in co-operation to realize them would be potential only. Indeed the underlying motive of love is precisely to do something for the satisfaction of the other, and its mutuality inevitably leads to functional co-operation. But there are important differences to be noticed. Since the association is not *constituted* by a common purpose, it permits of a change of purposes. In a partnership, if the common purpose is dropped or becomes unrealizable, then the partnership is at an end. Not so with a friendship. If the two friends drop one common purpose for which they co-operate, it is only to find another. In the second place, the common ends which are worked for and the co-operation for their achievement are together means to maintaining and deepening the friendship. From this we must conclude that in the nexus of personal relationship community is capable of generating and containing society within itself, of making the co-operation for the achievement of common ends a means to itself and an expression of itself. Therefore it is clear that if the problem of community is solved the problem of society will be well on the way to solution.

It still remains true that within limits at least society can be independent of community. Our two men can be partners and co-operate in the work of running their business without being friends. The necessity of making a livelihood, the pressure of immediate self-interest, may be sufficient motives to maintain the association. But there are limits to this. In the first place, though their co-operation is theoretically possible in the absence of friendship between them, in practice the absence of friendship limits the possibilities of effective co-operation in many ways; while if strong personal antagonism enters in, it may easily render co-operation impossible. It may simplify the issue if we remember that we are using the term friendship to draw attention to the whole range of forms of relationship which depend upon other-regarding motives; that is to say, upon motives which give rise to actions intended to affect the lives and fortunes of others. Such motives range from murderous hate, through a theoretical point of pure indifference, to the love which is ready to sacrifice life itself for the profit of the loved one. If we keep this whole range of behaviour in mind it is much less clear that functional co-operation is quite independent of the more personal forms of relationship of which friendship is our example. The more positive the personal interest the easier, *ceteris paribus*, the co-operation must be. The stronger the personal animosities between co-operating individuals the more difficult and inefficient the co-operation is likely to prove. It is only at the theoretical point of complete personal indifference that the co-operation is freed from the influence of the more personal elements in the nexus of relationship. Such an indifference is psychologically impossible between people who are in direct contact with one another. But it is possible and natural in highly organized societies, where very few of the individuals co-operating can know one another personally at all.

In the second place, any social organization is liable to be hampered or even disrupted by the intrusion of personal animosities. The machinery of co-operation seems to work smoothly only if the personal relations of the individuals concerned are kept, as it were, at a level of low tension. The more each one concentrates on doing his own part in the common task the better. The more the relations between them are determined by the common objective and the functional necessities of the plan of co-operation, the more efficient their efforts are likely to be. In all forms of organized co-operation, therefore, there is a tendency to look upon the more personal forms of relationship as a source of possible danger to the unity of the group. There is a latent tension between the two aspects of relationship. Society demands from it members a devotion to a common end which transcends all 'private' ends, and a loyalty which is ready to sacrifice both oneself and one's neighbour to accomplish it. But from the standpoint of community, such a demand is absurd and blasphemous. For its values lie within, not beyond, the nexus of relationship; and all co-operation is a means of expressing the common life. Persons, not purposes, are absolute.

It has been necessary to draw the contrast between those two forms of relationship in the personal nexus because it is vital to the problem of freedom.

Probably everyone to whom freedom is a practical issue would agree that it only becomes a real issue when there is oppression; when somebody is putting constraint upon someone else and so infringing his natural liberty. This is to recognize, of course, that the locus of the problem of freedom lies in the personal nexus. From this recognition it is a natural step to the view that the solution of the problem must lie in a reorganization of society which will order the relations of individuals in such a way that the tyranny of one man over another, of one group or class over another, is eliminated. All the great struggles for freedom have taken their stand upon this view. Yet when they have won their victories in the revolt against this tyranny and that and have established the new order for which they strove, the result has always proved a disappointment to the idealists. Freedom remained obstinately unachieved. Constraint and tyranny reappear in forms ever more complicated and more difficult to deal with. Today, after centuries of struggle and effort, it is at least doubtful whether all the progress made has not left the majority of men less free than they were in the days of serfdom and slavery; with a wider gap than ever between their reasonable desires and the satisfactions they can actually attain. This is not to say that there has been no progress. Progress has been immense and in spite of the pessimists is increasing its speed every year. The measure of progress is the increase in the range and complexity of what is objectively possible for man. This has risen so high that it is not absurd to say that already we are in a position to eliminate poverty from the life of mankind. But freedom is measured by the ratio between what is objectively possible and what we can actually achieve. It looks as thought that ratio is lower than it has ever been in the history of civilization. Two things seem to be true together in the strange period to which we belong: that man's power of achievement has grown vast beyond belief; and that his capacity to achieve any serious human purpose is diminishing at an alarming rate. It is an age at once of unparalleled effort and unparalleled frustration.

The reason for this paradox seems to me to lie in our failure to distinguish the two aspects of relationship in the personal nexus. Not only do we use the terms 'society' and 'community' more or less interchangeably, but we tend increasingly to think of the nexus of personal relationship as a nexus of organized co-operation. As a result we are bound to conceive the problem of freedom as a problem of social organization; and, since the central organ of social organization is the State, as a political problem, to be solved by political means. The effort to solve the problem politically can only have the result of producing the organization of tyranny in the totalitarian State.

For consider. If a man is primarily a function in an organized co-operation pursuing a 'common' purpose, then he exists for the group, as a means to the achievement of the common purpose. This is equally true of all his fellows. He and they have no more fundamental unity which might determine or modify or in any way challenge the social purpose. It is this purpose which determines them, sets them their places and their functions. Only in virtue of this organizing purpose are they a group. One is inclined to reply at once that this is clearly nonsense; and indeed it is. But we must not locate the 'nonsense' in the wrong stage of the argument. If human society were fundamentally a nexus of politico-economic co-operation, as so much of our modern thought and practice asserts or assumes, then any limitation of the claims of the group sovereignty upon the individual would be ridiculous, and any freedom for the individual would be accidental. The theory and practice of the totalitarian State are direct corollaries of this characteristic modern assumption. If, on the other hand, the individual has any ground of claim against the State; if it can treat him unjustly and deprive him of freedom which is his by right of nature; then he is not primarily a functional element in an organized co-operation. He embodies in himself, as it were, an authority which limits and defines the merely political authority of the organized society. Moreover, it is not as a mere individual that he can claim such an authority; as a mere individual he cannot even exist. It can only be as a member of a more primary nexus of relationships than those of any organized society, and in which the ground of all organized society is to be found. This is the nexus of communal relationship, which we here distinguish from the social nexus. We have thus reached the point at which we can say that freedom can only be maintained in this nexus of human relationship by maintaining the primacy of the personal nexus of community over the functional nexus of organized society. If this is secured, then no doubt a well-organized society will provide greater freedom for its members than an ill-ordered society. But the most perfect organizing of society, if it involves the primacy of the State, as the authority of organized society, must result not in the extension but in the obliteration of freedom.

The problem of human freedom is then the problem of that nexus of human relationships of which friendship is the type. It belongs to the field of our direct personal relationships; not primarily to the world of our indirect, functional, or legal relationships. This was the one point which I set out to maintain. I may well conclude by showing that this means that the basis of freedom is personal equality.

The essence of any friendship consists in the achievement, in it, of a real sharing of life, of an effective mutuality of experience. This involves, of course, material co-operation, as we have seen. It is in this effort to achieve such a nexus of relationship between ourselves and others that we have our most direct experience of freedom and constraint. Freedom is the result in so far as we succeed. Constraint is the penalty, as it is the proof, of failure. Freedom is the product of right personal relations. Constraint in the personal nexus is evidence that there is something wrong with the relationships involved. This 'rightness' in such relationships is in fact personal equality. If there is constraint in a personal relationship there is a failure to achieve and maintain equality. Unless people treat one another as equals they are not friends. If one treats the other as an inferior, then he is using him as a means, and the friendship ceases to be a friendship. Thus personal equality is the structural principle of relations which are communal in type, while the experience of freedom in relations is their characteristic expression. What throws the personal nexus out of gear, and so introduces constraint and limits or destroys freedom, is always a failure to achieve or maintain personal equality. In other words, what destroys freedom is the will to power. Where one man seeks power over others, where one class or nation seeks dominion over others, the denial of equality involved creates constraint and limits freedom. And there is no way in which freedom can be restored or increased except by overcoming the desire for power.

The conclusion is a negative one; and not particularly comforting. To all the plans for achieving or defending freedom by political or economic organization it comes as a serious and unwelcome warning. There can be no *technique* for achieving freedom. The field in which freedom has to be won or lost is not the field of economics or politics, of committees and rules. It is rather the field which has hitherto been the undisputed domain of religion. An age that has put religion aside without even recognizing the need to put something in its place has already lost the sense of freedom and is ripe for the organization of tyranny. On the other hand, the will to power, though it may affect an epoch like an epidemic, is still a disease. It is not natural. And it may help us back to health to recognize the disorder from which we suffer.

Nine

Persons and Functions

People and Their Jobs

G.K. Chesterton once wrote an article entitled, 'Should Shop-Assistants marry?' He had found the words, if I remember rightly, on a poster advertising some popular journal, and they had moved him to anger and to scornful denunciation. The proper question, he thought, would be, 'Should human beings, capable of love and marriage, consent to be shop-assistants?'. I agree with Chesterton. The two views of life which lie behind these two questions are opposite and irreconcilable. The first assumes that people are less important than the jobs they do; that men and women should shape their personal lives to suit their social functions; that the personal life is subordinate to the functional life. This view has made rapid progress in the last quarter of the century. Yet to accept it is to surrender the citadel of Christian civilization; for Christianity stands or falls by its great discovery that men and women are persons, and not functionaries of any earthly society.

I: *Two Ways of Life*

In these four talks I want to discuss with you the relation between people and their jobs; between human beings and their functions in society as carpenters, typists, engine-drivers, or housewives. We shall do this by contrasting the two views I have referred to: the Christian view and its antagonist. The Christian view is that

[1]   From 'Persons and Functions I–IV', *The Listener*, 26 (1941), pp. 759; 787; 822; 856.

the personal life is the important thing, while our functions in society are important only so far as they contribute to the personal life. Against this we shall set the view that the value of our lives consists in the contribution we make to the life of the society. This we shall call the functional view. Let us remember that these are not merely two theories but the expression of two ways of life. One way — the Christian way — subordinates the functional life to the personal life. The other way subordinates the personal life to the functional.

We shall start by trying to see the picture from the functional point of view. Functionally we are living organisms. The parts of our bodies have each their function. Every organ contributes something to the life of the whole. The continual harmonious working together of all these organs is our bodily life. If we are to live, the body must be provided with the conditions and the materials which it needs for its proper functioning: warmth, fresh air, food and drink. Nature has given us our senses and our intelligence to help provide for these bodily needs, and implanted in us the impulses which move us to use them. Of these the impulse to seek food, and the impulse to reproduce our kind are the two which shape our lives most strongly. These we share with the higher animals, as we also share with some of them the impulse to live in groups for protection and mutual aid. Clearly our biological life consists in the proper performance of functions.

But there is a clear gap between us and even the highest brutes. What constitutes this gap? I should put first the need we are under to work. Unlike the other animals, we cannot take what we need as we find it. We have to cook our food, make our clothes, build our houses. By nature we are workers. Next I put the power of speech with which is closely bound up the power to think and reason. Through this we can communicate with one another, and plan co-operation in work, organizing a division of labour. Some grow the food, others build the houses, others again put all their labour into making clothes; and the products of all are pooled and shared out to supply the needs of each co-operator. This is the natural human society. It is a co-operative society of workers, in which each has his function, which he performs for the whole society. If we look at this co-operative society as a whole, we see that it resembles an organism very closely. Perhaps this is why we sometimes describe it as the 'body politic'. Individual men and women have become, as it were, cells in the body of society, organized into groups which are the organs of social life, each with its function in the life of the whole body. Here many thinkers have found the secret of the transformation of the mere animal life into human life. Our capacity for co-operation has caught us up out of an individual existence into the wider life of a society which stretches back into the mists of history, and onward into an unguessed future which has perhaps no end. Our contribution to the greater life of society gives meaning and purpose to the insignificance of our individual mortality. We are human, they say, because we live *in* society *for* society. That is the functional view: the 'organic' view of human life.

We see, then, that the functional life is that part of our life in which we are making our contribution to the life of society as a whole. How much of a normal life does this cover? Clearly it includes all the working life by which we earn our livelihood. Can we say that this fills a man's functional life and that the rest of his life is his own personal life? I don't see that we can. Eating and sleeping take up a deal of our time out of working hours. I should call these activities functional: certainly not personal. Some people devote part of their spare time to social service of one kind or another. We can hardly exclude this from their contribution to the life of society merely because they are not paid for it. Is a man's home life, then, his personal life in contrast to the rest? To say this would hardly be doing justice to his wife. Has the woman who runs a home from morning to night no social function? Is the getting and rearing of children not a very important contribution to the life of society? Where indeed would society be without it? It looks as if the home life must also be reckoned as functional, and that the only activities which are left are in the nature of amusements and recreations. Even these, someone will tell us, are indirectly functional. They relax and refresh a man's mind as sleep refreshes his body, and so fit him for the next day's toil. If this be so, then we have come to an important conclusion. The functional life covers the whole of life. The whole life of the individual is his contribution to the life of society. From this point of view the meaning of our lives lies in their functional character. What gives us any human dignity or worth is the part we play in the life of society; and the good man is he who performs his function, or does his duty, faithfully and well.

II: *Subordination of Person to Function*

What would a human society which had fully realized this functional character be like? It will have the same structure as any typical public service. Think of the Post Office, for example. At its head is the supreme authority, the Postmaster General. At the foot are the common people: postmen, sorters and so on. In between there is a whole host of officials of higher or lower rank, each with authority over a larger or smaller group of subordinates; each with a superior whose orders he must execute. This is the picture of human society which emerges from the functional view of life. At its head stands the sovereign state, which is the supreme authority over the whole of life, because it is the supreme organizing principle. At the bottom are the working masses, whose duties are assigned by the state and who are organized by the state. Above them stands a hierarchy of officials of varying ranks. Since some functions are higher than others, men are emphatically not equal in such a society. The law of functional life is orderly subordination to authority, and obedience to the superior. Authority is not arbitrary: it is bound by functional laws. Its aim, however, and its standard are not freedom but efficiency; and the value of the individual as well as his dignity lies in his doing his duty in the task assigned to him in society.

Is such a society just a philosopher's nightmare? Would to God it were! It is the society of Hitler's Germany, and of the New Order he seeks to impose on Europe and the world. Perhaps you find this an astonishing conclusion to an argument which seemed to be moving bravely in the right direction. It is at least a sobering one, and I want to emphasize it rather than tone it down. You will land yourself in Hitler's camp if you hold strictly and ruthlessly to the principle that the thing that gives significance to man's life is his function in society. When we followed out this principle, we found no personal life anywhere. We found functions but no persons; politics, but no religion . . .

Fellowship in a Common Life

Last week we built ourselves a picture of human life on the assumption that the significant thing in a person's life is his social function. Now we have to start from the assumption that the centre of significance lies in the personal life. There is no part of life that has no function in the life of society. But there are few parts of life that are merely functional. The personal life is not 'other-than-functional' but 'more-than-functional'.

The most obvious of all functional activities is eating. It is the hallmark of our animal nature. Like animals we must assimilate food and drink periodically or we die. But wait a moment! Are we so like the animals in this? Animals feed. Human beings don't feed. They meet together at prearranged times round a table to share a common meal. There, it is true, each member of the family absorbs food and drink for the nourishment of his body. But that is only the foundation of the meal. And on this foundation humanity has always built one of the temples of the personal life. They would be strange people who lived on the foundations of their houses. I put it to you that a happy family, centred round the table for their evening meal is *not* properly described as a group of animals feeding. The family meal is a personal matter, built round a functional need. It is an occasion for meeting together, for enjoying the company of those we love. It is essential to the human quality of our eating and drinking that its functional basis should not come into the foreground. There are occasions when this happens: a man may 'wolf' his food when he is starving; for less natural reasons he may 'make a pig of himself'. When we yield to the temptations of the flesh we accuse one another of behaving like animals. This is to slander the animals. They cannot lose their innocence — not being persons. Debauchery is a prerogative of the personal life

I: *Unity Created by Affection*

Functionally, there is no difference between supper at a boarding-house table among complete strangers, and with your own friends at home. But personally they are very different. The boarding-house is deadly until you have made friends with your companions. Notice also how eating and drinking become the means of celebration. The impulse to say 'come and have a drink' to a friend you have met accidentally does not come from thirst. We invite people to have dinner with us, not because we are hungry but to show friendship. Under the old laws of hospitality, to treat as an enemy the man who had eaten your salt or broken bread under your roof was a monstrous sin. Feasts and festivals are occasions by which we express our loyalties, and our aspirations. So, imperceptibly, the personal meaning which gathers about our eating and drinking leads us into the religious field; where at the centre of our worship we find a sacred meal, a holy communion; in which the act of eating and drinking has become the pure symbol of the human and the divine. These reflections help to show us how a functional activity is transformed into a personal one. It becomes personal by becoming part of a common life. The family is united round the table. We partake — that is, take part — in it. The meal becomes an expression of fellowship, an act of union. The sacramental character which it reveals when we celebrate a feast is there from the beginning. All celebrations are occasions of expressing unity, comradeship, a mutual sharing of a common experience. Whether religious or secular, august or homely, they are all acts of communion. And what is fellowship or communion but the enjoyment of a unity created by affection? This indeed is the only tenable conclusion. The personal life is rooted in love.

It follows from this that the personal life is a life of mutual relationship not an 'individual' life. When we contrast the social with the personal life we are not contrasting a life in relation with other people with a life out of relation to them; we are dealing with two different kinds of relatedness. We are contrasting life in a functional society with life in a personal community. The functional life becomes social through an organized division of labour and a planned co-operation in work. But the personal life is a life of mutual relationship from the start. So let us dismiss the notion from our minds that the personal life is 'individual' or solitary. Love, which is its very essence, is inconceivable except as a mutual relationship. Indeed it is through our personal relationships that we become individual persons.

II: *At Home in the World*

How then shall we picture human life if we look for meaning in our personal rather than our functional relationships? Clearly, the home and the family life will have a central place, while the place of business will be somewhere on the circumference. It is in the home that the functional life with which we are born is transferred into a personal life. There we learn to use feet and hands and fingers, to walk and to speak. These are significant lessons. But the vital thing is that there we learn to love, in response to the love and care which supplies our needs. All of us learn this lesson with difficulty and very imperfectly; and it is this which makes persons of us. Love is no natural instinct. We are born perfect egoists, demanding and expecting that the whole world shall serve our pleasure. Love is the capacity to break out of this natural self-centredness and to care for someone else. It is the power to set our interest outside ourselves, to affirm not our own needs and our own pleasure but the pleasure and needs of someone else. In this there is involved the creation of conscience, of selfhood and of reason, since all these are based upon and express the power to be interested for its own sake in what is not ourselves. By learning to love we are taken into the common life of the family, and become persons in a personal community.

What then about the working life in society, the functional life which has its centres in factories and workshops, in the fields and on the seas, in shops and offices? From the personal point of view it exists to serve the personal life. Remember first that a home of some sort is the centre of personal life for every normal human being over the greater part of his life. In early times the family community was also the unit of working life. Nowadays we have separated the two for more effective co-operation. But still men go out to work, and come back home. They go out to work for their families. The maintenance of the family is the motive and meaning of the working life. From the personal point of view the whole network of economic life exists for the sake of the personal life which centres in the home. The state, with all its authority and power, is only a set of 'services' — civil services and military services — presided over by 'ministers'. If we ask 'whom do they serve, and to whose needs do they minister?' the answer is 'the people in their homes'.

So when we make the personal life the centre of significance the picture which grows up is not of a cooperative society of workers organized into a unity by an all-mastering state, but of a network of homes in which men share a common life, and which they serve and maintain by a social system of co-operative labour. This system is ordered and controlled by a democratic state, responsible to the people. But this is not the whole picture. The creation of personality by love is a process which is never completed. It goes on to widen and deepen the common life and our capacity to share in it. Beyond the home we seek new friendships which bind home to home in a wider community. We find new loves which establish new homes, linked to the old. In every contact with our fellows we see an opportunity to extend the range of our personal lives. In factory and office men who are brought together by the pressure of need, are ill at ease and resentful unless they can transform their partnership in labour into comradeship in life. So the links spread that bind man to man, and group to group, in the fellowship of a common life that points and moves towards the community of mankind. And here at last we find the place of religion. It is the unifying principle of the personal life of mankind, as the state is of its functional life. In religion the personal life has become the clue to all experience and to all reality. God is our Father, and all we are brethren. We are at home in the world.

Two Lives in One

We have distinguished two lives that we all live. There is the personal life, with its natural centre in the home, and love as its principle; and there is the functional life, with its centre in the workshop or the factory or wherever we earn our livelihood, and with its basis in organized co-operation. We have seen how the personal life gives rise to religion and moves towards the brotherhood of mankind; and how the working life gives rise to the state, and moves towards the creation of a world-wide system of planned co-operation. Now we must consider unity of these two lives. For the same people live both. We all have to reconcile the claims of both in our own daily experience.

I: *Personal Life Needs Cultivation*

I propose first to state the principle which governs the true relation of the two lives. Then I shall try to explain it as shortly as possible. Lastly I shall illustrate it. Here is the principle. The functional life is *for* the personal life; the personal life is *through* the functional life. I want you to hold this firmly in mind while I try to explain what it means. It holds the clue to everything else. The first half of this principle asserts that the functional life is *for* the personal. This means that a man's working life is for the sake of his personal life; that the meaning and purpose of life in the factory or office is to be found in the home life; that men are not to be used for labour, but labour is to be used for men; that people are more important than the jobs they do; and that religion is more important than economics and politics together. Not every one will agree with this. Someone will surely say: The personal life is important, of course, and we should make the most of it, for its own sake. But surely the work of the world and the man's part in it is just as important, and we should put all our hearts into our jobs while we are at them, and do them for their own sake. 'Surely', he will say, 'it is a mistake to make either of them subordinate to the other'. My answer to this is that we can't dodge the problem like this. It is not possible in practice to keep the two lives separate. The kind of working life a man has to live decides the kind of personal life he can have. The family that can just manage to make ends meet, so long as father doesn't fall ill or lose his job, is compelled by its functional conditions to develop a meagre and stunted home life. The personal life needs cultivation, and that means time and resources. We cannot keep the two lives in water-tight compartments because the shape of one decides the outline of the other. If the personal life cannot control the working life, it will have to fetch and carry for it.

The errors of thinking that the functional life has independent rights of its own appears in various disguises. 'Business is business', it says; 'you mustn't let sentiment interfere with business'. This is poisonous doctrine. The truth is that you mustn't let business interfere with sentiment if you want to save your soul alive. At other times we hear that religion should not interfere with politics. Then what, I ask, is the point of having any religion? This indeed seems to be the question that more and more people are

asking. And if anyone tells us that the church should be master in
the spiritual field, while the state should be master in the material
field, we shall answer — in the words of the Gospel — that no man
can serve two masters. The value of co-operation, of organized
work, is that it increases and concentrates power. It enables us to
do together what we couldn't do separately. To say that the functional life of organized society has an independent value is to say
that power is good in itself. But power is merely a means of doing
something. That is its only value; it *has* no value in itself. Yet the
misers think it has, and the money-worshippers, and the state-
worshippers and of course the world-conquerors and all the people who like to throw their weight about . . . After Hitler we may
be pardoned if we are a little fierce in asserting that the service of
organized society has no value in itself; that the functional is for
the personal.

But we must not forget the other half of our principle. The personal life is through the functional. We don't achieve the personal
life by escaping from work. The man who has no function,
whether he is an unemployed workman who can't get a job or a
wealthy parasite who won't, is cut off from the foundation upon
which the personal life must be built. I must recall here some of
our earlier discoveries. We found that the personal life is not
other-than-functional but more-than-functional. We found also
that the personal life is not individual. It is the life of fellowship;
that life that is shared. Its basis is love; and love means caring for
other people. The personal life is not the life of pleasure and play.
There is mirth and laughter in it, but even more certainly there are
tears and darkness. For love is measured not by what it gets but by
what it gives. 'Greater love hath no man than this: that he lay
down his life for his friends'.

Now friends need to do things together. How else can they
express their friendship? It is true that for love's sake people
invent things to do together which have no other significance
than to express their affection. They play games together or go
walking. But these charming frivolities don't take them very far
unless there are other more serious activities which they share. It
is only through sharing the burdens and troubles and labours of
life that friendship is made real. So it is over the whole range of
experience. Throughout the greater part of history the working

life of men and women has been held within the family. It is only yesterday that we began to separate the two, in order to achieve a larger and more intricate system of co-operation. But this does not alter the principle. If the next mass organization of labour is not to poison the springs of civilization it must be held within the human fellowship of the community, and must express its brotherhood. The personal life of the community must be realized through its functional life, or it will remain a statesman's peroration or a poet's dream. The principle of personal relationship is equality. If men are not treated as equals they are denied friendship. The principle of functional relation is subordination and inequality. If the inequalities of the functional life are not subordinated to the deeper equality of human fellowship, they become absolute, and community perishes.

II: *Relation of Love and Sex*

Perhaps this will suffice to explain the meaning of the principle which governs the proper relationship of the two lives. It runs, you remember, 'The functional life is *for* the personal: the personal life is *through* the functional'. But lest some of you think that the two halves of the principle contradict one another, let me illustrate it by reference to the relation of love and sex in marriage. Sex and love are not the same. In one sense they are opposites, with a tension between them. Sex is functional: the animal urge to reproduction. Its gratification is quite possible in the absence of love. Love is personal. It is indeed the very essence of personality. Yet there is something peculiarly inhuman, something peculiarly repugnant to our personal nature, in the idea of sexual gratification in the absence of love. We recognize instinctively that sex must be linked to love and subordinated to love. Without this subordination of the functional element to the personal, human marriage is impossible. We are not likely to make the mistake of thinking that sex has its own value, and should be cultivated for its own sake, because we know that, loosed from the service of love, sex becomes a cancer that rots the personal life, destroying the very capacity for love. Yet to separate love from sex, in the interests of love, is also an error. Love is through sex. The personal is through the functional. To talk of preserving the purity of love from contamination by bodily desire is to talk sentimental nonsense. Love unlinked to sex remains unfulfilled and unfruitful, a mere matter of feelings and ideas and talk. Only through sharing the material substance of life can love become real. It is through sex that love becomes marriage and creates the family, which is the first personal relationship in human life; as it is the source and inspiration of all the others. Here in marriage we see the simplest expression of our principle, and the unity of its two parts. Sex is for love, yet love is through sex. The functional life is for the personal life: the personal life is through the functional life.

The Community of Mankind

From the public point of view the functional life is the life of the state, while the personal life is the life of the community . . . I am using the term state, you will notice, in its popular sense and not in its strictly legal sense. The old-fashioned name for what I mean is 'civil society'. In this sense, then, the state is a functional society. It is an organized body of citizens. It is a secular society, with an economic basis, concerned with the material interests of its members. It is a political society. Its structure is defined by law and defended by force. Within the framework of rights and duties maintained by the state, its citizens co-operate for common purposes.

The community, however, is personal society. It is not created by law, and cannot be dissolved by legal pressure . . . It is by law that we are members of the state; but we belong to the community as persons (not as citizens) by sharing the common life. The community is a fellowship or brotherhood as it were. Its members recognize each other by a sort of family likeness; they feel a kind of spiritual kinship, an inner unity through which they 'belong together'. Clearly then community is not an organized, material, political society. It is rather a spiritual or cultural society. Its unity is in the widest, and in my view the solidest sense of the term, a religious unity.

We ought here to be able to speak of the church. For the peculiar unity of personal relationship which makes a community can only be properly expressed and nourished by religious institutions. But in our time the church seems to have lost touch with the common life, and nowhere in Europe is it now the symbol and organ of the community-life. Nothing has arisen which can properly take its place, but the need for some expression of the community has driven people everywhere to look to the state to undertake the duties of a religious institution. This is the origin of the totalitarian state, which is, indeed, simply a state trying to be a church as well . . . We must find the way to retain the true distinction, and the true relation, between the personal life of the community and the functional life of the state. What this means we shall discover if we apply our general principle to society. It will run thus: the state is *for* the community; the community is *through* the state.

I: Making Men a Means to Power

Firstly, the state is for the community. This is the principle of democracy. The state must be the servant not the master of the people. The state owes an absolute loyalty to the people in their common life of human fellowship. The economic system, and the political system which regulates it, have no value in themselves. They are there to play a necessary, but a subsidiary, part in the personal life of the community. The state has wealth and power and prestige; but these are worse than useless unless they are the means to a personal life of rich quality. If we remember the first principle of justice, that all men are equal before the law, then we can judge the value of the functional society simply. A good political and economic system is one which provides as fully as possible for the personal life of its citizens, and for all of them equally.

If the state refuses to serve and makes itself master of its citizens, it usurps an authority to which it has no proper claim. Democracy is not merely a form of society which we happen to like; it is the kind of society which is compatible with the dignity and the moral freedom of human beings. The totalitarian state is a blasphemy which demands that men should submit their consciences to its control. It may try to provide for the personal life, but it must fail. For it must invert the true values of life. It must make men a means to power . . . Why must it fail? Because the business of the state, as of all functional life, is power. The purpose of organization is to concentrate power. Where the state serves the community, its power is used by the community for personal, human ends. But if the state becomes master of the community, it can only use human life as a means to power. When power is thus made an end in itself it corrupts its possessor and drags its victims to destruction.

II: *The Real Atheism*

Against . . . totalitarianism, then, we have to assert the democratic principle that the state is for the community and not the community for the state. But this is only half of the principle: the other half is that the community is through the state. The personal life of society is through the life of organized co-operation. What unites a community is that its members share a common life. They are in sympathy. They understand one another. They have the same hopes and fears: a common past and common traditions. But this spiritual unity is only dream-stuff unless it is expressed in the sharing of our labour and our substance. It is through our co-operation in service that our community is made real. This working life produces a common stock of wealth; and this product of the common effort is the means which we possess, as a community, to care for one another. Our fellowship as a community only becomes real — only gets hands and feet — when in our daily work we provide for one another's needs and rejoice that we are doing so. When a man satisfies his own needs at the expense of another he refuses friendship, he denies community and lays the foundation of enmity and strife. When a group or a nation satisfies its needs at the expense of other nations, it does the same. All strife comes from refusal of community. This is why we can only escape from war when we treat the world as one community, in which all the products of the universal labour are a common stock to supply the needs of all men equally. In a true community, as in the family, the supply goes where the need, and not where the power, is greatest.

To bring to birth the brotherhood of man is the ancient purpose of the Christian Church . . . We see this not as a distant hope but as an immediate necessity. We shall have to learn to love our enemies, as Christ taught us, if we are not to destroy one another in the end. Is it too much to hope that the church may renew her failing life in the effort to achieve the world-community in our time? It is a religious task, demanding a religious motive and a religious leadership. It cannot be achieved by political or economic organization. The functional life is for the personal life. But neither can it be achieved apart from political and economic organization. The personal life is through the functional life. If the church is to perform its task it must conceive it in terms of the common working life of today, and not as a purely spiritual function. A faith in God which is not a faith in common humanity is an imaginary faith. The real atheism is the refusal of human brotherhood . . .

Ten

Self-Realization

It is usually unwise to interpret a catchword positively. A catch-word is a battle-cry, the symbol of an offensive, and its meaning is determined by opposition. 'Self-realization' is no exception. It is the battle-cry of a new idealism, and it is a call to arms. Its business is to rouse our emotions to take sides, to become partisan. If we are to respond, we must know first of all not what it stands for, but what it stands against.

The modern emphasis upon self-realization is a recoil from the demand for self-subordination, self-devotion, and self-sacrifice. It insists that our first duty is to ourselves, to realize to the full the potentiality of our own nature. It sets this duty in opposition to all ideals which find the value of human life in the service it renders to humanity at large, to a particular cause or a particular society, or to other persons. It would seem, therefore, at first sight to be essentially egocentric, anti-social, and anti-Christian, and it does undoubtedly reveal these characteristics in some of its phases.

But before condemning it outright, it would be wise to consider whether such characteristics are either a necessary or a natural part of a crusade against self-sacrifice. Even the staunchest admir-ers of self-sacrifice would agree that it makes an important differ-ence what a man sacrifices himself for, and whether the sacrifice is voluntary or unwilling. Many a man has sacrificed his life for his country in battle with the utmost reluctance, and the martyrs of pleasure-seeking are to be found in all the Spas of Europe. In this matter we clearly need a principle to guide us. Self-sacrifice is pal-pably absurd and immoral in certain cases.

Now no prophet of self-realization would waste powder and shot on a doctrine of self-sacrifice which nobody really believes

[1]   From 'Self-Realization', *The Expository Times*, 42 (1930), pp. 24–6.

in, and no one who believes in the virtue of self-sacrifice would admit that self-sacrifice is good in itself. We must be more explicit about the real issues if we are to understand what is at stake. The ideal of self-sacrifice which is challenged in the name of self-realization is really the attitude of mind which feels that society is more important than the individual, and which therefore believes that it is the duty of the individual to devote himself to the service of the society to which he belongs. Behind that attitude lies the whole weight of the romantic idealism of the last century, the whole influence of evolutionary thought and the ideals of progress which it has generated, the whole effort of humanitarianism and social service in its many forms. It is *this* that the ideal of self-realization challenges to battle. The self-realization of individuals is more important, it maintains, than the realization of social welfare or of social progress. It seems to me that this position is true and Christian, and that the ideal of social service is false and unchristian.

The great fallacy which underlies all ideals which bid us subordinate our own welfare to the welfare of society is as old as Plato's Republic, although it never dominated human life as it has come to do in our own time. In its simplest form it is the fallacy of applying mathematics to the things of the spirit, of thinking that the welfare of two men is more important than the welfare of one. In this crude form the absurdity of the assumption is readily apparent. A sorrow is not twice as great because two people feel it. Indeed, it is lessened if they bear it together in sympathy. We cannot add souls together, nor their experiences. An injustice is not less important because it is suffered by a solitary individual. The majority principle has no standing in the moral life, in spite of the ingenuity of utilitarians, for there is no experience which is not the experience of a single individual.

The first result of thinking that the individual should subordinate himself to the group because the welfare of the group is more important than the welfare of the individual is to produce an effective social materialism. For if human welfare is to be measured by numbers it must be measured in terms of that which can be multiplied and divided, and so bought and sold. This is by no means what the idealism of self-devotion to the service of society intends, but it is none the less its only possible result. The welfare of the group is something less than the welfare of the individuals composing it, not something more. For it is the welfare of the individual members in so far as that welfare can be produced and distributed among them by organized corporate effort. Only material welfare can so be produced and distributed, for it alone can be handled and managed statistically. And the group is a statistical conception. This helps us to understand the curious paradox of the history of the last century, to see why the lofty idealism of a Hegel becomes in practice the economic interpretation of history of a Marx, why the humanitarian movements degenerate into a national scramble for wealth and possessions, why a war to make the world safe for democracy ends in a peace of the pickpockets.

The second result of subordinating individual welfare to social welfare is that in effect it sacrifices persons to organizations. This is inevitable. It is organization which turns a mere multitude into a society, which therefore we *contrast* 'self' and 'society', when we distinguish the welfare of the individual from the welfare of society, we are in reality contrasting persons with institutions. If we imagine that the individual is of less importance than society, we are effectively asserting that institutions are more important than persons. The service of society consists, in fact, in serving people in the mass, impersonally. It consists in maintaining, improving, and elaborating the organization of society. The service of society and the service of others are essentially different activities. They do not come to the same thing in the end. The one is personal and involves personal contact and personal interest. The other is impersonal and is best done in an office, by statistics. If, then, we generalize the service of society as an ideal of human conduct, we are demanding of every man that he should look upon himself as a means to the maintenance and improvement of social institutions. We are denying the intrinsic value of human personality, and exalting the impersonal organization of life as the end which personality should serve. From a moral or religious point of view, this is a hideous thing to do.

We can now see the real meaning of the attack upon 'self-sacrifice' in the name of 'self-realization'. The personal must not be subordinated to the impersonal. The spiritual must not be sacrificed to the material. So far from being anti-Christian, the cry for self-realization echoes the central doctrine of all Christianity, the absolute value of the individual person. Men must not serve institutions. 'The Sabbath was made for man, not man for the Sabbath'. Society exists for the realization of selves, not selves for the realization of society. Is it really possible to imagine Jesus exhorting His disciples to devote themselves to the service of the Roman Empire, or to sacrifice themselves for the cause of Jewish nationalism? I think not. Nor can I believe that it would have made any essential difference to Him if He had been confronted by the British Empire and the League of Nations. Yet by a masterpiece of strategy the Prince of this world might seem almost to have persuaded the Protestant Churches to identify their Christianity with the defence and maintenance of the earthly societies of which they are members.

From this point of view, at least, the ideal of self-realization is fundamentally Christian. It insists on the supreme value of the individual person. Yet for most of us it retains a flavour of self-centred egoism which we cannot associate with the teaching of Christ. There can be no doubt that in the minds of many of its modern adherents self-realization and self-assertion are close companions. 'Am I my brother's keeper?' they seem to say, 'I have my own life to live. Why should I bother myself about anyone else?'. Such an attitude betrays a gross misunderstanding of the nature of selfhood. It is a psychological law that 'He that saveth his life shall lose it'. It is one of the conditions of self-realization that a man shall not keep himself locked up within his own heart. Self-realization is the true ideal of human life, but it demands an understanding of the nature of the self and its reality.

The characteristic of the reality of selfhood is its objectivity. Our own reality is not self-contained. It consists in our capacity to realize the independent existence and value of what is not ourselves. To be ourselves we must live beyond ourselves. If we misapprehend the character of the world in which we live, we are infected with illusion. The unreality that results is in us, not in the world outside us. It is *our* unreality. The more real our apprehension is of what is not ourselves, the more real we are in our own selfhood. This is the essential nature of personality. To realize ourselves, therefore, is to realize the world that is not ourselves. The self which is indifferent to the nature and significance of what is other than it, is indifferent to its own reality and cannot realize itself. This is obvious in the field of pure knowledge, where error is at once a failure to realize the self in its capacity as knower, and a failure to grasp the nature of that which we seek to know. But it is equally true and more important in the field of desire and emotion. To set our desire or our affection upon any object is to endow it with value and significance. If the object really lacks the value we assign to it, if it cannot sustain the significance we put on it, we are deluded in our emotion and in our desire. The delusion is *our* delusion. The unreality which it generates is an unreality in us, and it frustrates our own self-realization. Thus any failure to live in and by the reality beyond us is a destruction of the reality of the self. All egoism is deliberate self-frustration, for the self which shuts itself off from its other shuts itself off from the possibility of its own realization.

To this we must add another important factor in the problem. Since the self must realize itself in and through its other, the limits of self-realization are the limits of the reality of the other. In particular, the self can only realize its personality in and through another person. The self-realization of persons is a mutual thing, possible only through the fellowship of love. The self cannot be real in isolation, because the reality of persons is a mutual reality. This is the first wisdom, and to grasp it is to destroy the illusion that self-realization is an egocentric and anti-social ideal. On the contrary, it brings us straight to the new commandment of the gospel that we should love one another, and to the first principle of Christian metaphysics, that God is Love.

Each of us stands, in unescapable isolation, over against the whole universe in its infinite otherness. Yet in mere isolation from it we are absolutely nothing, completely unreal. To be real at all we must somehow pass beyond ourselves and enter into fellowship with the world. In doing so we become ourselves and remain ourselves. This continuous flow of our life beyond itself into the world, into fellowship with its other, cannot be a one-sided transaction. The flow must run both ways. We must take the reality which lies beyond us to our own hearts. It must give itself to us in a mutual fellowship. This is the law of our being. We find our reality in the love of other men and women. Our friendships are the nodal points, as it were, the centres of concentration of our own

reality in its self-transcendence. Yet in their isolation they too are
only points, these friendships. They depend for their reality on
the infinite beyond them. Through the love of men and women
our individual selves reach out to fellowship with the whole infinite otherness of the world which is not us, yet in which we live
and move and have our being. If this fellowship is to be possible
— and its possibility is the condition of our own reality — then the
infinity that stands over against us must needs be a personal God.
For God is the postulate of our own being; and our self-realization
is the realization of God.

Eleven

What is Religion About?

One possible answer to the question 'What is religion about?' is that it is about the salvation of the world. If I begin with it, this is not merely because it is familiar and has the authority of the New Testament behind it, but even more because it is so pertinent to the present condition of human society. We live on the brink of disaster. Any morning we may wake to find that armies are on the march, and a war that may end our civilization has begun. If ever the world needed saving it is today.

We all know this: but we also think of it as a political problem, to be solved, if it can be solved, by political means. We look, if not with much confidence, to statesmen as possible saviours. This is a mistake. The salvation of the world — as has been common knowledge in wiser ages than ours — is not the business of politics, but of religion. The salvation of the world is indeed the present-day problem; but it is a religious, not a political, problem: and religious problems can no more be solved by political action than a broken bicycle can be mended by prayer. Religious problems need religious solutions. Perhaps this is why all the energy and intelligence and goodwill that have been mobilized since the end of the first world war to create peace and security have seen our situation grow steadily worse.

[1]   From 'What Is Religion About? I–IV', *The Listener*, 56 (1956), pp. 916–17; 984–5; 1027–8; 1073–4.

I: *Where Rousseau Went Wrong*

There is a historical reason of our tendency to seek political solutions for religious problems. The Romantic movement, with its doctrine of the natural goodness of man, taught western Europe to look to a change in social conditions for the abolition of evil. Rousseau, glorifying the natural and the primitive, set going a programme of salvation by political revolution. To preach that man is good at heart, that human nature does not need changing, is not merely to deny a traditional Christian doctrine; it is to imply that there is no need for religion at all. But, by and large, we accepted the romantic teaching, and the result has been twofold. It suppressed the sense of sin; and it set religious objectives for politics. Freedom, equality, brotherhood, for instance: these are religious notions. To set political machinery at work to realize them is to make certain of failure; and the more wholeheartedly a government devotes itself to their pursuit the more likely it is to achieve their opposites. By what laws can men be constrained to love one another? What political compulsion will make us lay aside self-interest and suspicion, and treat one another as equals? A state with religious objectives is a totalitarian state. In one of his more candid moments, Rousseau admitted that in the society of his dream those who would not obey the general will would be forced to be free. We have seen recently what this means in practice in Hungary.

It seems to me a matter of great urgency that we should recover our sense of proportion and our sanity by discovering afresh what religion is about. By this I mean that we should bring to mind again that aspect of common everyday human experience from which religion arises and to which it refers. For then there is a chance that we shall cease to thrust upon politicians — or on scientists or business magnates — tasks which neither politics nor science nor industry is capable of performing; and look in the right direction for our salvation.

To discover what religion is about, we must look at what is characteristic of all religions at all times. We must disregard the things that belong only to some religions under particular circumstances. Such notions, for example, as these: that religious experiences are mystical; that religion is concerned, essentially, with the supernatural, or with another world, or with a life after death;

that consists in a set of beliefs about the world which may conflict with scientific knowledge. These ideas are true of some religions at some times; and we have a natural tendency to identify religion with the particular forms and associations of religion which we ourselves have known, particularly when we were young. We must try to counteract this tendency by looking for what is characteristic of every form of religion at any stage of human development.

I should like to direct your attention, therefore, to four general characters of religion, all of which are related to its universality. First: religion is a universal human activity. No society is known, however primitive or however developed, which is innocent of religion. In the history of civilization religion has played the role both of an integrating and of a disrupting force; and has proved its power as both a warmaker and a peacemaker. In our own time, the partition of India, like the partition of Ireland, has its source in religious differences which the plainest dictates of political desirability and of economic self-interest have been powerless to overcome. We may welcome this or deplore it; but we cannot ignore it. Only one inference is permissible. The fact that religion is a universal human activity must mean that it is rooted in some universal human deed and expresses some feature of human experience which is common to all men under all conditions.

Secondly, and closely associated with this: religion is uniquely human. It has no proper analogue in animal behaviour. Analogies there are of our arts and our technologies, like the blackbirds singing and the engineering of the beavers. But religious behaviour is peculiar to man. This must signify — must it not — that the universal experience which gives rise to religion must itself be uniquely human. It must be an aspect of our experience which we do not share with the animals. If it is true that what distinguishes man from the animals is rationality, then religion must be an expression of reason: by no means, as some have thought, irrational.

Consider now, in the third place, another side of this religious universality. Religion is the original matrix from which all the varied aspects of culture and civilization have been derived. In primitive society the elements of law and politics, of the arts and the sciences, of industry and technology, of morals and manners, are all fused together. They form a single system of custom in which the different elements are inseparable. And this unity of common life is expressed and conserved by religion. Primitive religion is the original, all-embracing expression of man's capacity to reflect. It is, that means, the primary expression of reason. We might state this in a historical form. All the various aspects of human activity, we might say, are derived from religion. In the process of social development these aspects of life grow distinct and strong within religion, and ultimately, one after another, they break loose, and establish their own autonomy. Usually the first thing that happens is a distinction between the material life of the community and its spiritual life. Originally there was one leader who was both priest and king. Now there are two; a priest to direct its spiritual activities and a king to rule its material ones. Religion then becomes one aspect of life instead of the unity of all the aspects.

II: Unifying Function of Religion

Even so, religion continues to have a unifying function so long as it remains vigorous. A true community is not held together by force. It has an inner, spiritual unity. A common temper and attitude pervades every aspect of its life, both private and public. It is the business of religion to express, and so to maintain and strengthen, this inner unity. If religion weakens and loses its influence, then this unity of spirit is gradually dissipated — though the force of habit may sustain for a time its outward show — and, with the loss of the unity of its aspects, society loses its sense of significance. People no longer feel that their community means anything or stands for anything in particular. This, indeed, is what we mean when we talk of a loss of faith; and this is why the decline of religion is the surest sign, as it is the natural accompaniment, of social decadence.

There is yet another aspect of the universality of religion to be noticed, which we might describe as a universality of intention. The religion of any human society is for every member of its group, and every member is compelled, or at least expected, to participate in it. Contrast this with science, for example, or with art. The people who take part actively in producing one science or one art are a small number of peculiarly gifted, and therefore unusual, individuals. Ordinary folk may be moved — to delight or repulsion — by the productions of the artists; they may be much affected, whether as beneficiaries or as victims, by the discoveries and inventions of the scientists; but they are not expected, nor indeed are they able, to participate in such doings. But every single person, from childhood onwards, can partake and is expected to partake in the religious ceremonial of his community. Thus religion has a democratizing influence. It makes all men equal before God. In most historic communities every member must participate in the established religion. Where religious toleration has been secured, everybody is still expected to participate. Moreover, in the development of religion there comes a point where it is recognized that only a universal brotherhood of mankind can satisfy the religious need. From that point onwards, the great religions appear, with a world-wide appeal, and seek to incorporate all men everywhere in their communion.

These are the four general characters of religion which we should bear in mind when we ask, 'what is religion about?' and set out to discover the aspect of common experience from which religion springs and to which it refers. They set the conditions which the answer to our question must fulfil. For any answer which is incompatible with them must be false; and any answer which fails to account for them must be at least inadequate.

What is Religion About — II

To the question 'What is religion about?' there is a simple answer which many of you must have thought of: Religion is about God and our relation to God. This is a proper answer to one meaning of the question. But it is another meaning that I have in mind. Last week[2] I put it like this: 'What is that aspect of our common experience from which religion arises, and to which it refers?'. I want to hold to this meaning of the question here. Whatever else religion may be, it is something that people do. So we can ask, 'What makes them do it?'. What is it in their ordinary lives which has drawn people, from the earliest beginnings of human life, to create religious ceremonies, religious rituals, religious duties? In a word, what are the facts to which religious symbols refer?

We have noticed four characteristics of religion. It is universal in human society; it has no analogue in animal behaviour, but is

[2]   In a talk printed in *The Listener* of December 6.

peculiarly human; it is the original matrix of all the aspects of human experience; and it seeks the participation of everybody in its ceremonial. The aspect of our experience which gives rise to religion must have corresponding characteristics. It must be an aspect of our lives from which the other aspects derive, and to which they return. It must be so common and so human that it is central in every human life, however primitive or however cultivated. What aspect of our lives can satisfy these conditions?

I: *The Inner Core*

My answer is this. It can only be that aspect which we call our personal life. For on the one hand, the personal life is the inner core, as it were, of our human existence, in which we are most wholly and most fully ourselves. We contrast our personal life with our public life, which we live in the world as workers or as citizens. These public aspects of our lives are impersonal; yet at the same time they are important parts of our lives as persons. My social function — my work — is to teach philosophy in a university. Is that part of my personal life? Yes and No. In one sense it is not. For it is arranged for me: I have to lecture at certain fixed hours; and I do not choose the people who come to listen. I am part of an institution, and when I retire, someone else will be found to take my place.

Yet in another sense it is part of my personal life. I find a personal satisfaction in the work I do; it has its source in my personal interests and abilities; and it is sustained by personal relationships with pupils and with colleagues. This has another side to it as well. Our impersonal or public activities are *for the sake of* our personal lives. If a man's personal life is a failure, nothing can make up for it. The most brilliant successes in the public life will be spoiled for him: he will find them pointless, insipid, and unsatisfying. This seems to fit the conditions we laid down. So we are entitled to say that religion is about the personal life.

But what is our personal life? There is a common tendency to think of it as 'individual', 'private', or even 'solitary'. This is wrong. For the personal life is first and foremost a life of relationship: it includes our family life, for instance, our friendships and our enmities too. The personal life has its solitary phases; its characteristic rhythm, indeed, is one of withdrawal and return —

withdrawal into solitary reflection and meditation, followed by a return to contact and communication. But the solitary phases are the negative ones. They enrich the return to fellowship, and this is their significance. We may make a further step and define the personal life as the life of friendship. It follows that religion is about our personal relationships.

This may be clarified by contrasting our personal with our functional relations to people. Functional relations are those in which we co-operate to achieve a common purpose. Think, for example, of a factory which makes typewriters. It consists of a team of people. There are workers of different kinds, as well as managers and clerical staff. Together they form an organized group. Everybody has his own particular task: everybody 'does his bit' and all the 'bits' are designed to fit together like the parts of a machine. So each one makes his contribution to the final result.

In such a team the relations between the people concerned are impersonal. They are, we might say, the relations of the jobs they do. The people needed in our typewriter factory are not certain unique individuals, but people with certain skills, type-founders and machinists, packers, carriers, cashiers, and typists. Every one of these can be replaced by another with the same skill, one typist by another, one machinist by another machinist. It does not matter *who* they are, so long as they can do what is wanted. So the relations of the people in our factory are merely functional. Some of them may not know one another; some of them may be friends; others may be enemies; but from the point of view of the production of typewriters all this is irrelevant. What matters is that each should do his own work and do it properly and at the proper time.

II: *Unique Personal Relations* —

Our personal relations, however, are unique. As husbands or wives, as parents, as brothers, or as friends, we are related as persons in our own right: and we are not replaceable. If I lose a friend I lose part of my own life. This is not a mere poetic metaphor. For we are what we are through our intercourse with others; and we can be ourselves only in relation to our fellows. Personal relations, moreover, are necessarily direct. We cannot be related personally to people we do not know. We must meet; we must communicate with one another; we must, it would seem, be alone together.

'Two is company', says the proverb, 'three is none'. In functional
relations this is not so. I am related by the work I do to a multitude
of people whom I do not know and shall never know. My tailor is
related functionally to the people who wove the cloth that he
makes up for me; but it is unlikely that he knows them. He may be
a friend of mine, but he need not be. Our relations may remain
impersonal; and though I must meet him, we may confine our
relations to the necessities of the service for which I pay him.

There are other differences between our personal and our functional lives. A personal relation is not created by a common purpose, and it is not dissolved if the common purpose disappears. A
group of friends will no doubt do things together. But this
co-operation does not produce the friendship. Our personal relations have no purpose beyond themselves, and what we get out of
our friendships is precisely friendship; which is what we put into
them. If this were not so we should be false friends, furthering our
private interests deceitfully under a cloak of affection, pretending
friendship from an ulterior motive. From this there follows
another difference. Personal relations cannot be organized, or
planned, as functional relations can. We do not enter upon them
with part of ourselves, or from one of our interests or with one of
our particular skills. The whole of ourselves is engaged, for better
or for worse. We have to give ourselves to our friends; and in our
relations with them we care for them, not for ourselves. We must
trust them, and hope they will be true to us: but we can ask for no
guarantees; nor can we make conditions. We have to commit ourselves, and expect the others to reciprocate: but if they will not,
there is nothing that we can do about it.

III: – and Their Problems

Personal relations have their own difficulties: they produce their
own perplexities and their own problems. These, as we all know,
are peculiarly painful and distressing; but also they are different
in kind from the problems of the functional life. If I find that one of
my friends is losing interest in me, there is no specialist that I can
call in to revive the warmth of our relationship. The problem of
the personal life cannot be solved by organization; they are not
technical. You can organize a factory but not a friendship. This is
the reason why it is so absurd to attempt to solve religious prob-

lems by scientific or political methods. Yet this is what our confusion of religious with political objectives leads us to attempt. We imagine that all problems can be solved if only we can discover the proper techniques. When we get into difficulties, we think we must be doing things in the wrong way. It may be that we are doing the wrong thing.

If personal relations have no purpose, why do we have them? If to love someone is to risk frustration and sorrow and disappointment, why do we do it? What creates and maintains our personal relationships? What disrupts and destroys them? The only answer to such questions is that this is our nature. We need one another. We need one another functionally, because there are so many things that we cannot do for ourselves or get for ourselves without the help of other people. But also, we need one another personally; because it is our nature to love and be loved. We need to care for others, even to spend ourselves for their sakes. This, in fact, is the most fundamental and the most characteristic of all human needs; as its satisfaction is the fullest and most absolute of all satisfactions. We talk and we behave as if this were not so. We try, for some obscure reason, to evade the issue. We pretend, even to ourselves, that we are above such childishness. We set ourselves to seek fulfilment and satisfaction in functional achievements, and let our personal lives atrophy and drop away. Why this should be so I cannot tell. A poet has called the fear of love our last cowardice; and in our lack of courage we pretend to ourselves that we can do without affection. Yet we cannot wholly succeed in our self-deception; and the complete egocentric — the man who really cares for nobody but himself — is either a monster or a maniac.

The truth is that we need others in order to be ourselves. All things seek the fulfilment of their own nature; and it is the nature of man to live beyond himself; to find the centre of his interest in the world outside; to care for what is other than himself. In thought and knowledge we call this self-transcendence 'objectivity'; but this is only one aspect of it. At its fullest it is the self-transcendence in which we care for another person with our whole being, and find our freedom and our fulfilment in him. Need I prove this? Who is there so ignorant that he does not know it, so poor in experience that he cannot recall a moment when there was no shadow between himself and a loved one, but only a complete trust and mutual revelation? In such experiences we know that we are most fully ourselves and most completely free. And so long as the illumination of such occasions stays with us, we cannot doubt that it is our nature to share ourselves with others and to realize ourselves in a community of life. Yet how rarely it happens; and perhaps this is the greatest paradox of human life. When any two human beings meet it is natural that they should enter into personal relation and care for one another as friends. It is, I say, the most natural thing in the world; yet it hardly ever occurs. This is what religion is about.

Why does it happen so rarely? Because we are afraid. We are full of deep-seated, half-conscious fears that will not allow us to trust one another, or to give ourselves away. We have learnt the arts of self-defence; to keep ourselves to ourselves, to give others no handle against us. We are on guard against being hurt – by other people's indifference or clumsiness or malice. We have learnt that people can be fickle, self-centred, and ungenerous. Our fear builds defences round us to keep people at a distance. But they also keep us at a distance from people, and so make friendship difficult and, in its higher reaches, all but impossible. The price we pay for our self-defence is that we can rarely be ourselves. Religion is also about this fear.

For most people the life of personal relationship centres into the family; first, in the family into which they were born, and then in the family created by their own marriage. It would be proper, then, to say that the family is the primary religious fellowship. For it is constituted by the personal relations of its members and sustained by their care for one another. It is also the original human society, from which all the other forms are derived. In the development of civilization the functional groupings for common purposes proliferate more and more. Yet all of them are for the sake of the personal life; and it is for the sake of wife and children that a man goes out to work and to war.

In the family, tensions arise. There is anger and conflict; enmity usurps the place of love; and instead of caring for one another its members feel the impulse to hurt and to wound. These tensions will make the family life a misery if nothing can be done about them; in the end they will destroy the family if they are not overcome. So there is need for peacemaking, for reconciliation, for forgiveness, for the renewal of trust and affection. It must be possible to blot out the past and make a new beginning. These are the foundation problems of our human existence. If they cannot be cured there is no hope for us. For if the personal life is sick there can be no wholesomeness in any of our activities. To describe these evils and their antidotes we have to use the language of estrangement and reconciliation, of forgiveness and renewal, of trust and hope and love: and this language is itself sufficient proof that these things are what religion is about.

The Celebration of Communion

In my first two talks[3] I have been discussing what might appropriately be called the facts of religion. I took our question to mean 'What is the aspect of common experience from which religion springs and to which it refers?'. The answer we found was this: religion is about the personal aspect of our lives, about our personal relations; about friendship and the fear of friendship. In consequence, the primary religious institution is the family, in which we learn to be persons in relation, and which is itself a unity in the bond of affection and the original of all human society.

In the next two talks I shall interpret the question to mean 'What does religion do about the facts to which it refers?'. I shall answer this question by discussing the two major aims or preoccupations or functions of religion: the celebration of communion and the creation of a universal family.

The celebration of communion is the central act of the Christian religion. That much is clear. But what does it mean to celebrate something, and what kind of this is it that we celebrate? Suppose that a group of us have been working hard together to get a particular candidate elected. The results have just been declared. Our man is in. As soon as we hear the news someone is likely to say 'Let's celebrate!'. And what do we do? We go and have dinner. But we do that every day; and no doubt during the campaign we have had dinner together more than once. Yet this is a special dinner — a celebration. It means something different. Our question is, however: What makes the difference? In what does the 'cele-

---

[3] Printed in *The Listener* of December 6 and 13.

bration' consist? And connected with this is another: What sort of
thing is it that calls for celebration?

We can best find the answer by considering simple forms of
human community. Take first the family and consider the relations of husband and wife. Their relation is a personal one, and
they live a common life. But this common life is a co-operation in
which husband and wife have different functions. The husband
goes out every morning to work and returns in the evening. The
wife stays at home, looks after the house and the children, provides for the family meals, mends the family clothes, and so on.
This co-operation — husband and wife each doing his own work
for the family day after day — is their common life. But in the evening, when supper is over and the dishes disposed of, and the
children in bed, they will sit down by the fire and talk about the
day that has ended; recalling its trials and its successes and sharing them with one another. This also is part of the common life,
but it is a curious part; for it is *about* the common life. It is not a
functional part: they are not now each doing his own job: they are
sharing the common life in recollection and each, as it were, is
making the other's part his own. Thus in their common life there
are two elements: there is the fact that their life is a common life;
and there is also for each of them their consciousness of the common life. They not merely do live a common life; they also know
that they do. This knowledge — this common consciousness of the
common life — is part of it and transforms it. It means that they
know that they belong together and in that knowledge are at one.

The difference that this knowledge makes is important. It transforms what is matter of fact into matter of intention. This is what
distinguishes any human society, however primitive, from an
animal herd. Both groups are united in a common life. But the
members of the human group are conscious of their common life,
and this knowledge make their unity intentional. It is maintained
by deliberate effort. It persists only so long as its members persist
in their intention to maintain it. It is held together not by any herd
instinct (if indeed human beings have any instincts) but by loyalty
and affection.

From this it follows that the greatest danger by which any community is threatened is an internal one. It is not that its food supply may fail or that it may be attacked by enemies, but that its

members may cease to make the effort to maintain the common life; that the will to unify may grow weak. For the other dangers can be faced and fought provided everybody stands together in a common will to overcome them. But if the intention to maintain the common life is lacking, the community is defeated in advance.

It is not to be wondered at, then, that every human society finds means to develop, sustain and intensify, in its members, the intention to keep the unity of the common life. These means are its religion. The activities of primitive religion — and on this issue we do well to keep our minds upon the simplicities of primitive life — have this simple function. They rouse and give expression to the consciousness of community in its members; they emphasize their sense of belonging together and surround it with expressions of honour; and by so doing they stimulate and strengthen the intention to maintain the common life.

The way religion achieves this is significant. It takes an element in the common life and invests it with a special significance. It may be singing or dancing or eating and drinking together — something that is already a normal part of the life of the community. But for this purpose the song becomes a sacred song, the dance a sacred dance, the meal a sacred meal. This 'sacredness' is expressed by a certain solemnity with which these acts are performed, and by a fixed and recurrent mode of performance which turns them into ritual. They become ceremonies. They have a special meaning attached to them which is not their everyday meaning: they are done not for the normal purpose merely but for a special purpose. What this meaning is we have already seen. These religious rituals are parts of common life which reflect and express the consciousness of the common life. They are, in fact, celebrations. This is why, in primitive life, the right to take part in these religious rituals is the hall-mark of full membership of the community. Strangers are excluded.

I: At One in Community

From this, too, it is clear that what is celebrated in such rituals is a network of personal relations which binds together, in a personal unity, all the participants. In performing the ritual the participants represent to themselves and to one another that they belong together, that their whole life is a common life, that they are at one in community. So the ceremony expresses, and in a sense is, their communion. To this we must add for completeness that these religious ceremonies are characteristically associated with the expression of joy and delight. Even rituals attached to death or disaster have this character. By joining together to express their sorrow or their fear they objectify it. It becomes a grief that is shared, and the sharing already softens it, and the ritual expression beautifies it; the expression of personal unity outweighs, without denying, the grief that occasions it. We may conclude, then, that this primary function of religion, which we have identified as the celebration of communion, consists in a common activity which expresses for all the participants the knowledge that they are united in a common life, and their joy in this knowledge. This common ceremonial, it is easy to see, must have the effect of reviving and enhancing the sense of community and so strengthening the intention to maintain the common life.

There are two corollaries to this conclusion which should be noticed. The first is that the primary aspect of religion is the performance of a common ritual ceremony. It consists in doing something and doing it together, to express the knowledge that we are united — not in idea, not in the religious act, but in the community of an everyday life. The second is that the attitude of mind which is the opposite of the religious attitude is individualism. In its primary character, religion is not a set of beliefs: neither is it about the individual or for the individual. It is about relationship: it is for the sake of community.

I should like, in conclusion, to indicate why it is that this primary aspect of religion contains in itself all the other aspects not merely of religion but of human life as a whole. We have said that religion expresses and reinforces the consciousness of the common life. If there is to be a consciousness of the common life there must already be a common life to be conscious of: and this common life consists in working together to provide for the common needs and in facing together the dangers which threaten. To be conscious of it and to express that consciousness means to recognize and to contemplate the conditions of life, both material and spiritual; to represent to ourselves the problems we have had to share in the past and which we shall have to face together in the future.

So if we celebrate our fellowship we do something that involves remembering the past and anticipating the future: we represent to ourselves, in symbol and idea, both what has been and what will be. To do this is to think; to use our past experience to envisage the future; and so to plan in advance the solution of future problems. Since this life that we share in common is the whole life and the totality of its conditions, there is no aspect of life, whether spiritual or material; there are no conditions of life, whether natural or personal, which may not be called to mind and thought about when we remember and express our fellowship in living. This fact makes religion the matrix of all reflection; and this is why every aspect of life and culture is included in primitive religion, whether morality or law, politics or economics, art, science, or technology. For all these are brought to consciousness in the celebration of communion and we are apprehended as parts of the one experience of human fellowship. In this way religion reveals itself as the primary expression of human rationality and the source of all the forms of reflection, both theoretical and practical.

In this religious reflection which we have called the consciousness of community, there are two sets of conditions which are of special significance. The first set centres in the family and concerns the relations of the members of the family to one another. The fellowship of the family draws its structure and character from the facts of birth, marriage, and death. It is a fellowship of young and old. The fellowship of any human community belongs to what Plato called 'the world of coming into being and passing away'. In this field the celebration of communion makes us remember our dead and anticipate a time when we ourselves shall be no more. To be conscious of our membership of a community is to realize that we are born and die while the community remains. Thus the consciousness of community enlarges the bounds of community to include the dead and those as yet unborn. And in strengthening the intention to maintain the community it makes it possible for us to co-operate in the interest of a future which we ourselves shall never see. It is this aspect of reflection which gives rise to all the forms of ancestor worship, and finally represents God as the universal Father.

The other set of conditions concerns the relation of the community to the natural world. The community depends upon and co-operates with Nature. All efforts to provide for the common needs are fruitless without the help of the earth and the sun and the rain. This dependence, too, is brought to mind and symbolized in the celebration of communion, and the various forms of nature worship are the result. In this direction also the fellowship is enlarged, and man enters into communion with Nature. In the maturity of religion these two aspects are brought together and the Father of all men is also the Creator of the world.

II: Our Activities as Expressions of Fellowship

I have kept your attention upon primitive religion for the purpose of simplicity. In closing, let me say that in its highest reaches the core of religion remains the celebration of communion. The aspects of experience which are fused in primitive religion have been separated out and have established their autonomy. Politics and industry, commerce and technics, the sciences and the arts are pursued by different groups of people as if they were ends in themselves. It is the business of religion to gather these disparate activities together by gathering us, who pursue them, together to become conscious of our community and to celebrate our communion. If religion is effective, we pursue our different occupations not for their own sake but as elements in the common life, and we discover their meaning as embodiments and expressions of a fellowship in which we all care for one another. But if religion fails to do this, then the life of our societies becomes a thing of shreds and patches, of bits and pieces without relation or structure, meaningless and empty.

The Universal Family

The celebration of communion is one of the two universal functions of religion. The other is the creation of a universal family, and it is to this function that I shall devote my final talk. Like all things human, religion is not born full-grown, and its primitive stages do not fully express its nature and functions. We have therefore to distinguish between primitive and mature religion. Primitive religion is primitive because of its limitation, which is the limitation of the community which it celebrates. The development of religion indeed is hard to distinguish from the development of society; not because it is an aspect of social development, but because the development of human society is itself a religious development. Why this must be so we have noted previously. What makes a human group human is the consciousness of the common life, and religion is the expression of this consciousness. In some sense, the development of human community depends upon a development in the consciousness of community, and so on a development of religion.

I: *The Bond of Affection*

A primitive society is based on blood relationship; it is a kinship group; though we should remember that this includes its dead. Consequently, its religion is confined to those who are blood relations. Blood relation is mere biological fact: but, as we saw, a human community is a matter of intention. To put it otherwise, what constitutes the unity of a family is not that its members are in fact related by blood; but that they care for one another, and so hold together. These two things — the fact of blood-relationship and the personal bond of affection — have no necessary connection. Blood relations may not love one another; and groups of people who have no natural kinship may be bound together in friendship and form a community. So from the earliest times there have been ceremonies of adoption, by which a stranger is made a member of the kinship group. The adopted child is counted a member of the family though he is not so by birth; and this means that membership does not necessarily depend on blood relationship.

The first stage in the development of religion is the discovery of this, and of its implications. Since religion is always concerned with the consciousness and the intention of community, it will inevitably come to define community in terms of consciousness and intention, not of biological fact. The implication is that any group of human beings can form a community — can be brothers in a family, since any two people can be friends. Consequently, there are no limits set by natural fact to the membership of a human community: they are all limits of consciousness and intention. All men, therefore, can be brothers and the human family is potentially universal.

The first great stage, then, in the development of religion runs from the primitive tribal religions, each sanctifying the fellowship of its own kinship group, to the emergence of the universal religions. A universal religion is one in which the idea of the universal family, of the brotherhood of man, has been brought to consciousness. The second great stage will run from the emergence of the idea of a universal brotherhood to its realization. For it is a profound mistake, though a common one, to imagine that religion is concerned only with ideas and beliefs; only with propagating the idea of the universal family and not with bringing it into being. Karl Marx, indeed, thought that religion was the popular form of idealism. On the contrary, idealism and religion are at bottom incompatible. For real religion, human brotherhood is not an idea to be contemplated but a task to be achieved.

Even in primitive society the function of religion is not limited to the celebration of communion. Within the common life animosities arise, so that friendship is broken and needs to be restored. One member may do injury to another or to the whole community, and restitution must be made: or a group within the community may become alienated from the rest, and then there is a need for reconciliation and atonement. Religion has therefore the task not merely of celebrating the communion that exists but also of restoring the communion that has been broken. It must concern itself with all the disturbances of personal relations, and learn to overcome them. It must discover and learn to use the means for turning hatred into love, for overcoming jealousy, eradicating malice, substituting for self-interest a will to serve the community. In a word, it is the business of religion to effect the transformation of human motives. What makes this possible is that it is natural for people to be friends, and where they are at enmity it is because of fear. This we have considered: now we may add that the supreme problem of religion, and therefore the supreme problem of human life, is the overcoming of fear.

We see now why the methods of religion and of politics are so different, and even antagonistic. Politics must take human motives as they are, and find means to maintain social co-operation even between hostile and self-interested groups. In the end, it must appeal to self-interest and use the threat of compulsion, which is itself an appeal to fear. But religion must never accept human motives as they are; its task is to change them. It cannot be satisfied with an external unity of co-operation; because its business is to achieve an inner unity of mind and spirit, a fellowship of affection.

For a universal religion this aspect of its function — the restoration or the creation of fellowship, where it is absent — must become primary. For it implies an actual community of people whose communion it celebrates. But this actual group is possessed by the idea of the universal community of mankind, and has voluntarily accepted the task of realizing it. Consequently this religious group thinks of itself as potentially universal; as the present representative of the coming community of the world. It intends, not its own existence as a limited and independent group, but its own transformation into the universal family.

II: An Open Society

The methods it can use for achieving this objective are dictated by the nature of its problem. It must be an open society. This means that any human being can become a member of it if he will. No difference which is mere matter of fact — like race or nationality, colour or sex, for instance — can be a ground of exclusion. Anyone who remains outside does so because he refuses to come in. That is the first condition set for it, because the moment it excludes anyone, except by his own refusal to join it, it ceases to intend a universal community. The second condition is that the community must reject the use of force, either to extend its own membership or to defend its own existence. The reason for this is a simple one. You cannot compel people to be friends; you cannot remove the fears that stand in the way of friendship by an appeal to force. It must be, therefore, a free society, where there is no compulsion to membership, a society which is constituted by the fact that its members care for one another and this 'caring' must be real, not a matter of ideas or feelings but practical and material. In relation to the world outside also it must be unafraid; never on the defensive. In a word it must be the kind of community of which no one *need* be afraid; all the fears which keep people outside it must be unreal and unnecessary.

Such a human community, by being potentially universal, by refusing to defend itself, and by caring openly and actively for all its members, can offer its fellowship to all men everywhere with a sound hope of success; since what it exhibits in its own life, and what it offers to others, is the answer to the deepest and most personal need of any human being — the need to love and be loved. It can prove the *bona fides* of its offer by caring actively and disinterestedly for those outside it in their human needs. To see this is to understand two of the most famous injunctions of the Christian Gospel, the injunctions to meet injury with forgiveness and to love your enemies. These are not high ethical ideals. They are simple common sense. They are the only means and the necessary means for the task the Christian community has undertaken. For if we meet injury by insisting on our rights — on penalties and reparation — we perpetuate the break in fellowship which the injury produced. If we refuse to meet hostility with love, all hope of transforming the enmity into affection, and so of extending fellowship, is gone. The principles of what is sometimes called the Christian ethics are simply the rules for creating the universal family. We fear them because they demand of us a total objectivity — an objectivity not merely of thought but of emotion and of will.

So we return to our starting point — that religion is about the salvation of the world — but with a fuller realization of the means to that end, the self-devotion of a religious community which has abandoned security in order to create a common life and a common fellowship of all mankind. Something like this, though imperfectly and with mixed motives, was accomplished by Christianity in the Dark Ages, when it created the unity of Christendom, which transcended then, as it still transcends, the boundaries of all the political unities within it. Today events are thrusting us rapidly forward towards some kind of effective world unity. In the present medley of traditions and nationalisms and conflicting political creeds this unity, if it were forced upon us, could take only one form — a military dictatorship wielding overwhelming force, a sort of universal Roman empire. It could not be a free democratic unity, because the possibility of democracy depends upon a common way of life. Co-operation may be produced by force and fear. Community needs a common intention grounded in the conviction, in all its members, that they belong together in the unity of a fellowship. That is why I began by saying that religion is about the salvation of the world. To this I add that the only way of salvation for the world is the creation of the universal family.

Twelve

Prolegomena to a Christian Ethic

It has been for many years a hope of mine that I might find the time to formulate, in a systematic fashion, the ethical teaching of the New Testament, and particularly of the Gospels. This would be a major undertaking, and what I write now falls far short of this. But it is not unrelated to it; for it arises from repeated, if unsystematic, reflection upon the conditions of fulfilling such a project. Certain problems have presented themselves for solution which I cannot solve. Certain possible conclusions, between which a choice must be made, compete with one another for acceptance. Certain valuations which seem to differentiate the teaching of the Gospels from other ethical attitudes have focused themselves in my attention, without achieving systematic relation to one another. It is something of all this that I have in mind to express; no firm conclusion, certainly, but rather certain *prolegomena* to any conclusion which may eventually become possible.

Firstly, there is a very real question whether there can indeed be such a thing as a Christian ethic. One's answer to this question depends greatly upon what one means by an 'ethic': and this might seem to be a question of words. But it is much more than this; as indeed most questions about words, if they give rise to controversy, must be. For the meanings we give to words — the ways in which we use them — depend upon our place in real situations. Most of us, I suppose, think of an 'ethic' as a system of principles, or rules, in accordance with which everyone ought to

[1]   From 'Prolegomena to a Christian Ethic', *Scottish Journal of Theology*, 9 (1956), pp. 1–13.

behave. A Christian ethic would mean, in that case, a formulation of the rules, principles or laws in accordance with which a Christian should live; and since a Christian must claim that these rules are part of the truth, they must, it would seem, be the valid rules of conduct for all men under all circumstances. What I wish to draw attention to here is the connexion, in our minds, between the idea of the ethical and the idea of acting in accordance with a law; which, as a moral law, is both universal and obligatory. The idea of doing one's duty, of recognizing a moral obligation which binds us to act in certain ways, whether or not we are so inclined, is another, perhaps a more formal way of expressing the same conception.

In *this* notion of a Christian ethic there are two assumptions which call for examination. In the first place there is the assumption that the Christian way of life is the right way of life for everyone; that the rules of a Christian ethic are the universally binding moral rules, whether this is recognized by the non-Christian world or not. Now I find this assumption a doubtful one. It seems to me possible that principles of Christian behaviour, if such can be formulated, may be rules for carrying out a special purpose, the salvation of the world; and that they are then obligatory only on the *ecclesia* (Church) or those who are chosen and set apart for the service of this purpose: in the first place the children of Israel — the chosen people: and in the second, the Church, chosen from among all the nations when the Jews, rejecting the Christ, had refused to carry out their mission.

Take, for example, the teaching in the Gospels about forgiveness. Any Christian ethic must surely contain a rule of forgiveness, as the proper way of behaving in the face of injury. Now to forgive an injury is not compatible with punishing the guilty party. One cannot have it both ways; if I ought to forgive, then I ought *not* to demand reparation. If this principle is universally binding, it is incompatible with all punishment, with the recognition of civil law, and indeed, with the very existence of the State. But it may well be binding upon a special group of persons who have voluntarily accepted the task of reconciliation. As a means to reconciliation the rule of forgiveness is simply common sense. For if two of us are at enmity and the injured party desires a reconciliation, the only way open to him is to forgive the other. To insist on justice, or to demand reparation can only serve to perpetuate and to embitter the alienation which he deplores. Seen from the point of view of a mediating group — the Church — whose function is reconciliation, many of the so-called 'ethical' teachings of our Lord, far from being ideal standards of human behaviour, are common sense indications of the necessary means for accomplishing a specific task.

If one were to accept this view in general, it would imply that Christians are committed to a type of conduct which is not obligatory, as a universal ethic, upon men who are not chosen for the Christian task; and that their commitment to this way of life follows logically from their special function — as the necessary means to the end which they seek to realize. Such a position reminds us of the double standard of behaviour recognized in medieval thought — though that holds as between clerical and lay members of the Church. We may also recall that Jesus recognizes a 'righteousness' of the Scribes and Pharisees which is not good enough for His disciples.

This is the first of the preliminary questions which must, it seems to me, be faced by everyone who wishes to formulate a 'Christian' ethic. It seems to presuppose different moral levels, relative to different conditions or functions; and to imply that any Christian ethic there may be is an ethic binding only on members of the Church, and not on other men.

The second assumption that should be examined is, I think, one which goes deeper and is of more consequence. Is the notion of acting in accordance with rules — the idea of duty and obedience to a moral law — compatible with Christianity? If it is not, and if this is what is formulated in an ethic, then there can be no Christian ethic. If then a Christian ethic is to be possible, we must accept one of two alternatives. Either Christianity can provide us with a moral law which we must obey; a set of duties which as Christians we are under moral obligation to perform; or else there can be an ethic which dispenses with the idea of law, duty and obligation.

We must, I think, reject the first alternative. If there is a Christian ethic, it is not thinkable in terms of duty and obligation. My reasons for this conclusion are as follows: First, it is characteristic of the teaching of our Lord, as we find it in the Gospels, that He does not formulate general rules of conduct. His 'command-

ments' are not general moral rules. 'Be ye perfect, as your father
which is in heaven is perfect'; this is clearly not within our power
to perform. If 'ought implies can', then this cannot be a duty. 'A
new commandment I give unto you, that ye love one another'. To
this the moralist will reply, 'I may have a duty to act as if I loved
my fellows. I cannot have a duty to love them'. This avoidance of
the form of law in His teaching cannot have been other than deliberate. For the idea of the law, and of obedience to the law, is characteristic of the whole of the Hebrew tradition in which He was
brought up. It seems to follow that to reverse this and to formulate
a Christian ethic in terms of general rules of Christian duty is to
miss something that is characteristically Christian. The Pauline
conception that we are freed by the Gospel from the law, and from
the hopeless attempt to obey the law, does clearly reflect what is
characteristic of the Gospel teaching. To formulate a Christian
moral law *is* 'to be entangled again with the yoke of bondage'.

In the second place, though the idea of duty is conspicuous by
its absence in the Gospel teaching, there *is* one little parable of
which it is the theme. The farmer coming home from the fields
with his servants does not invite them to supper with him. No, he
tells them to get him his supper: after that they can have their
own. Jesus comments on this, 'So likewise ye: when ye have done
all things that were commanded you say, We are unprofitable servants; we have merely done our duty'. Like the righteousness of
the scribes and pharisees, doing one's duty isn't good enough!
This comes very near to being a categorical rejection of the morality of duty.

Finally, it is clear that a Christian ethic, if there be such a thing,
is an 'ethic of love'. This means that it is based, not upon reason
but upon emotion. (I use this contrast, not as approving it, but as
appropriate to any discussion of the morality of obedience to
rule.) The ethic of duty, both in its ancient Stoic form and its modern Kantian, explicitly depends on the suppression of feeling as
the motive of action in favour of a 'pure rationality'. It is, therefore, in principle, incompatible with an ethic of love. Kant is at
pains, you will recall, to distinguish ethical from pathological
love in order to square the command to love one's neighbour with
his notion of obedience to the command of reason. Kant wishes to
say that 'loving one's neighbour' means acting 'as if' you loved

him. Pathological love is simply love that *is felt,* in contrast to a benevolence which is *thought* as obligatory. The Kantian ethic, then, resting on a totally different principle from the Christian ethic, is incompatible with it.

We are then thrown back upon the second alternative — if we are to have a Christian ethic — that the idea of an ethic is not necessarily bound up with the notion of obedience to rules, and that the ethic which is organized, as by Kant, round the idea of duty or moral obligation, is only one type, and not necessarily the correct type of ethic. Can this be allowed? It seems not merely that it can, but that it must; if only because classical Greek ethics, as we find it in Plato or Aristotle, is, at least as much as Christianity, innocent of the idea of duty and of the ideas of 'the Will' and of 'the moral law' which are bound up with it. Whatever our judgment may be upon the value or the validity of the classical Greek ethic, it would be very peculiar to deny that there is such a thing. After all, it was the Greek philosophers who invented ethics. If we are prepared to use the term 'ethics' to include the moral theories of Plato and Aristotle, then there can be no objection to talking of a Christian ethic, on the ground that it is incompatible with a morality of rules, the notion of duty, or the conception of a moral law. On this issue Greek and Christian stand together. (It may be urged that the Greek has not yet reached the idea of a moral law, and that Christianity has gone beyond it. I have no inclination to deny this; but it is irrelevant to the present issue.)

At this point I should like to speak for a little, not as a Christian but as a moral philosopher, about the three types of ethic which I find it necessary to recognize. But before doing this there are one or two points I should like to mention which may make it easier to follow my argument, and which may provide a transition from the first section of my prolegomena to the second. The first point is this. If we can agree that there can be a Christian ethic which does not rest upon the idea of obedience to rules, and requires not a 'rational' — which means really intellectual — but rather an 'emotional' basis, then the first ground for doubting that there can be a Christian ethic is much weakened. That doubt rested upon the consideration that the moral demands laid upon the Christian might be relative to his special task; so that they could not be universalized as binding upon all men. But this demand for an absolute ethic, applicable to all men, is clearly itself bound up with the idea of a system of rules universally obligatory. If this sort of ethics is not necessarily the only sort; if there can be an 'ethic of love' which is not an 'ethic of law' then much of the force of the first objection is lost.

The second point I have in mind is one which makes clear something that has already been implicit. When people talk about a Christian ethic, whether they are Christians themselves or not, they tend to mean a set of moral beliefs which have become traditional in the teaching of the Western churches, that is to say, in the Roman Church and its Protestant offshoots. We tend to assume, somewhat gratuitously, that there is an ethical orthodoxy which has remained stable, except perhaps in some relatively unimportant details, throughout the centuries of Christian history. This view is tenable, if at all, only at a high level of generality; through the sort of abstractness which enables some moralists to maintain that the differences between all systems of morality are minor and inconsiderable. The closer we approach to the substance of actual living, the greater and the more glaring become the contrasts between the 'ways of life' which the Christian churches, at different periods of history and among different peoples, have sanctified and sought to maintain. But even if there were such an orthodoxy, it would be necessary to distinguish between the ethic of Christendom and a Christian ethic. What we habitually denote by the term 'Christian morality' is so mixed with conceptions drawn from Greek philosophy, Roman law and Old Testament sources, that if we took it as our *datum* our first task would be to distinguish within it what is Christian from what is pre-Christian or pagan. Yet to make such an analysis we should have to know already what distinguishes a Christian from other types of ethic. My personal view of the ethic of Western Christendom, for what it is worth, is that it is, in the main, not Christian but Stoic.

Speaking now as a student of moral philosophy, I wish to maintain that what essentially distinguishes one ethic from another is not a variation in the general types of conduct which they approve or condemn. It consists rather in two related factors; first, the attitude to life which underlies and sustains them; and second, the distribution of emotional emphasis within each. This second factor is simpler to deal with, and easier to understand, so we may dispose of it in a few sentences before tackling the other, which is more difficult. What is meant by 'the distribution of emotional emphasis' is this. The types of conduct which are disapproved by any ethical doctrine are condemned with very different degrees of moral repugnance. Likewise the virtues which are esteemed are felt to be praise worthy with differing intensities of approval. Some offences are venial and are readily forgiven; others know no forgiveness. This distribution of emotional emphasis varies greatly; and can be measured by the social penalties which attend the breaking of the code in this particular or that. In seeking to determine, then, the unique peculiarity of a particular ethic, one of the first questions to be asked is this: 'What is its unforgivable sin? What sort of moral offence does it consider the most serious?'

Turning now to the first factor which I have mentioned — the attitude to life which underlies and sustains a particular ethic, we face a more elusive issue, which is also, in a broad and fundamental sense, emotional rather than intellectual. An 'attitude of mind' — or as we may call it more technically, a 'form of apperception' — is the fundamental subjective factor determining human behaviour. The objective factor is a knowledge of the facts. We act in a situation through knowledge of the situation. Even if our knowledge of the facts, however, were comprehensive and exact — as of course it never is — this in itself would not suffice to indicate what should be done. For that a valuation is required which goes beyond the facts and which selects an objective. Thus the same facts can be taken in different ways. A serious difficulty to be faced which will stimulate one man to wrestle with it and overcome it, may bring discouragement and despair to another. This difference depends, not on what the facts are, but on how they are taken, envisaged or *apperceived*. Apperception is really a form of selection by concentration of attention in terms of a predominant interest. The way things 'look' to us depends upon this selection.

Now most apperception is empirical: by which is meant that the interest in terms of which we attend to a situation is one we have acquired in the course of our experience. But there are three forms of apperception which deserve to be called categorial, in that they anticipate particular experience and belong to the original structure of human nature. Thus they determine the form of *all*

human experience. For all of us, the original structure of experience involves complete dependence upon another human being.
In consequence the original and the primary reference of these
categorial forms of apperception is to the relations between persons. They dictate the possible ways of taking (or 'apperceiving')
our relations to our fellows: and since these inter-personal relations are *in fact* the central organizing principles of human life,
whether we admit this or are even aware of it, the categorical
structure of our relations to other people determines our relation
to the 'Other' in general, that is, to the world.

In its most formal expression, our relation to our fellows may be
either positive or negative, either one of attraction or one of repulsion. These two opposite attitudes may be identified through
their most mature expressions in personal life in the antithesis of
'love' and 'fear'; but it is important to remember that these two
terms must be taken in the widest possible sense. Indeed as
categorial they determine the form of our experience in general
and are consequently normally 'unconscious'; not elements
within our experience. The detailed analysis of them is out of
place here, even if it were particularly relevant. The distinction,
for our purposes, may be best expressed if we say that two opposite attitudes of mind are possible towards any set of conditions in
which we must act, one of trust and confidence and one of distrust
and suspicion. The latter, if it is dominant, throws us on the defensive and dictates, as our general (if unconscious) objective, security. The former is best defined by contrast as the opposite of this,
in which behaviour in relation to the Other is spontaneous, free
and unconstrained.

It may be well to consider at once a point which has considerable importance for all ethical studies. If we are to talk about what
is 'natural' in human behaviour, then we must say that the positive, trustful and confident attitude is 'natural' to man, while the
negative, defensive attitude is 'unnatural'. This is sufficiently
shown by the fact that the purely negative relation, if it were
unchecked, must aim at the destruction of the relation either by
the destruction of the Other or of the self; either by murder or by
suicide. Nevertheless this natural state is very far from being the
actual state of human relations. We are therefore fallen beings; in
whom there is evident a loss of their true nature. But this loss is

not complete; otherwise the only relation possible between people would be Hobbes' war of each against all, resulting in the self-destruction of the human race.

There are three, and not two categorial forms of apperception because of the ambivalence of the negative attitude. Negative attitude to the Other necessitates a policy of self-defence. But this may either take the form of a withdrawal from the Other or of aggression against the Other. If I fear someone I must either conceal myself from him or secure power over him. Now, in general, I cannot actually withdraw from my relation to the world, since my life consists in this relation. What I can do is to conform to a pattern of habitual activity which the Other accepts, while finding my real life within myself, as a life of the mind, of the imagination, or as it is often called, a spiritual life. In this attitude to life I conform to the demands made upon me by the world; I submit to the Other, but only in fact, not in intention. My real self is not involved in my material activity but is 'withdrawn'. The alternative to this is a self-assertion which seeks power to compel the Other to conform to my demands; and so compels the Other to do likewise.

Now these three possible attitudes to life tend to give rise to three different types of ethic; and where one of them is dominant in a cultural tradition it will actually do so. The positive apperception, because it provides a motive for realizing personal relations of trust and confidence is itself constitutive of a fellowship in community. The two negative apperceptions tend to the destruction of fellowship; as they are inherently self-centred. Nevertheless, because social co-operation and social confidence is necessary to human existence, they must give rise to some form of behaviour which makes social cohesion possible in spite of the tendency to personal antagonism which underlies it; and to do this they must base their ethic upon the self-interest of the individual agent.

The two negative apperceptions give rise to two types of ethic with which we are familiar. The defence by submission and withdrawal produces an ethic of good form; of conformity to an accepted pattern of social behaviour. This is really an aesthetic notion, which makes morality the Art of Living. From the standpoint of the individual, the good life is achieved by a balanced and harmonious satisfaction of the natural impulses in such a way that a man's life as a whole is as it were a work of art, satisfying to contemplate. From the social side, individuals are the elements out of which an organic social whole is realized: each, like any element in a work of art, has a function in the life of the whole, and his goodness consists in the performance of his function. This ethic seeks to combine these two points of view through a process of education which 'forms' the character of the growing child so that the pattern of its habitual life fits the function he is to perform, and so that his vision of the good life for himself is that which his society requires. This conformity becomes automatic; and what satisfies the individual also serves the community.

The other negative apperception — that of defence by aggression — seeks security through power. Now if power is the end aimed at, since power is just the general term for the means of achieving anything, the attitude to life must be a technological one. Its ethic, therefore, is a technological ethic. Practical achievement comes through discovering and acting upon rules. It requires above all the capacity to maintain a policy; and to subordinate one's momentary satisfaction to the attainment of a practical objective. The corresponding ethic, then, must be an ethic of *self*-control; and the good life must be one which is lived in accordance with the right rules, that is to say, in obedience to the moral law. This is the familiar ethic of acting from duty; of doing what we ought to do and not what we want to do. It dictates a morality of obligation.

This may serve, I hope, to identify the two types of ethic which I have in mind; and at the same time to clarify what I mean by a difference of apperception. I have introduced this rather abstract discussion, indeed, not for its own sake, but to provide a contrast with the apperception that underlies the teaching of the Gospels, and to which any Christian ethic, if there be a Christian ethic, must conform. It is to this contrast which I wish now to draw attention. The first point, and perhaps the most fundamental one, in the contrast is that both these negative types of ethic assume that the tension between individuals, and the resulting tension within the individual between impulse and moral demand is 'natural' to man, and an unchanging condition of human existence. Consequently they envisage the moral problem as one of making personal intercourse and social co-operation possible in spite of the underlying impulses which threaten it. In contrast to this, Christianity refuses to recognize this enmity which arises from fear of the Other as natural, though it recognizes it as actual. Consequently, the moral problem is not one of countering the effects of the destructive tendencies in us in one way or another, but instead the problem of eliminating these tendencies themselves. Christianity finds men at enmity with one another and concludes that which is required is a reconciliation. It thinks in terms of regeneration, of the salvation of the world, of the transformation of human motives. The natural state of man is one of fellowship in love and trust; if that is not his actual state then something has gone wrong which ought to be put right; which must on no account be accepted as proper, or natural or normal. We might perhaps express the contrast by saying that to the question: 'Why can we not do as we please?' the Christian answer is: 'Yes, why can't we? Let us find out and put it right'.

This contrast in apperception seems to me to be the first consideration which should underlie any attempt to formulate a Christian ethic. If we believe that human motives can be transformed, the whole conception of right action or of good conduct is affected. The good life is neither a life which exhibits a harmonious unity of structure, nor one which conforms to certain eternal principles. It is the life of fellowship: and actions are right as they contribute to the creation, the extension and the maintenance of fellowship.

With this there is bound up another aspect of the contrast. Because fellowship is the good, a Christian ethic cannot be egocentric, as the negative types of ethic are. Fear necessarily makes the self the centre of reference, and goodness an achievement which in some sense or other satisfies the self. But love transfers the centre of reference beyond the self to the Other and action which expresses love is for the sake of the Other, not for the sake of the self. It is a mistake which flows from the negativity of our own normal apperception, when we say that Christianity teaches the infinite value of the individual. It would be more correct to say that from a Christian point of view the individual has no value in himself as an individual, but only in relation to God and therefore in relation to his fellows.

I should, perhaps, refer to the evidence there is in the New Testament for this whole treatment of the subject. There is first, the continual contrast, in the teaching of Jesus, between fear and faith. I find this sufficiently striking to make the contrast serve as the definition of faith — as that state of mind which is the contrary of fear — not the logical contrary which is courage, but the psychological which is trust or confidence. I should even be inclined to say that our Lord considers fear to be the condition from which we require to be rescued. This is confirmed when we remember that a major theme of His teaching is the utter condemnation of the defensive attitude to life. The parable of the talents is, perhaps, its most extreme expression. It is the man who played for safety by burying his talent who is cast into outer darkness; and this has its fullest formulation in the statement that he that saveth his life shall lose it. This may suffice to indicate the direction in which I should look for justification of my suggestion that the positive form of apperception in my analysis is in fact that which underlies and so conditions any possible Christian ethic.

Since our own dominant ethic is the ethic of law and duty, it is perhaps proper that I should consider, if only tentatively, whether the contrast I have drawn completely excludes the idea of duty and of moral law from a Christian ethic. I find myself wishing to stand with St Paul on this, when he says 'All things are lawful for me; but all things are not expedient'; and when he goes on to relate this expediency to the conscience of the weaker brother. Put in the language of the schools this means, I believe, that the Christian attitude is incompatible with a belief in absolute and unchangeable moral laws. An ethic of love cannot *be* an ethic of law. But there is room for such an ethic to make use of rules; though these must be relative and changeable. Above all it must be quite wrong to think that it is possible to substitute an ethic of duty for the ethic of love; or to formulate rules of conduct which express the Christian view of what constitutes good behaviour. The reason is simple enough. In any personal relation the bond of unity lies in the fact that we behave to one another in the way that expresses our care for one another. To substitute for this conduct which is determined by a rule, and so to act dutifully, is to put an end to the fellowship. Rules, however, may be useful, provided they are, in St Paul's term, rules of expediency. The ethic of duty as obedience to a moral law rests upon a confusion between moral value and politico-economic value; and the morality of form and function confuses moral with aesthetic value.

I said earlier that types of ethic were differentiated not only by the form of apperception which sustains them, but also by the distribution of emotional emphasis within them. I should like to conclude by using this test to differentiate the Christian ethic from the other types we have discussed. To do this I should refer to the violent condemnations drawn from Jesus by what He called the 'hypocrisy' or 'play-acting' of the Pharisees.

This type of behaviour seems to qualify fairly well as that moral evil which is, from the Christian point of view, the most unforgivable. In what does this vice consist? In 'acting a part', or in 'playing a role'; that is to say, in behaviour which is calculated and not spontaneous, in which the way we behave does not flow from and express our real state of mind. It is a sort of insincerity in behaviour, which has the effect of concealing the real man from those with whom he comes in contact. As compared with this sin, the sins of the flesh are venial, and easy to forgive. This distribution of moral emphasis seems to me a distinguishing characteristic of any possible Christian ethic. But my main purpose in drawing attention to it is this. The other two types of ethic we distinguished make morality itself a systematic play-acting; for both, though in different ways, are concerned to achieve a type of outward conduct that conceals and disguises the real character of the inner life. And this is indeed inevitable, since they accept the enmity between men as natural, and yet seek to produce, in public, the semblance of fellowship.

Bibliography

Key Works by John Macmurray

Freedom in the Modern World (London: Faber, 1932; repr. with an Introduction by Harry Carson, Atlantic Highlands, N.J.: Humanities Press, 1992).

Interpreting the Universe (London: Faber, 1933; repr. with an Introduction by A.R.C. Duncan, Atlantic Highlands, N.J.: Humanities Press, 1996).

The Philosophy of Communism (London: Faber, 1933).

Creative Society: A Study of the Relation of Christianity to Communism (London: SCM Press, 1935).

Reason and Emotion (London: Faber, 1935; 2nd edn, 1962; repr. with an Introduction by John E. Costello SJ, Atlantic Highlands, N.J.: Humanities Press, 1992; reissued, 1995).

The Structure of Religious Experience (London: Faber, 1936).

The Clue to History (London: SCM Press, 1938).

The Boundaries of Science: A Study in the Philosophy of Psychology (London: Faber, 1939).

A Challenge to the Churches (London: Kegan Paul, 1941).

Constructive Democracy (London: Faber, 1943).

Conditions of Freedom (London: Faber, 1950; repr. with an Introduction by Walter Jeffko, Atlantic Highlands, N.J.: Humanities Press, 1993).

The Self as Agent (London: Faber, 1957; repr. with an Introduction by Stanley M. Harrison, Atlantic Highlands, N.J.: Humanities Press, 1991; reissued, 1995).

Persons in Relation (London: Faber, 1961; repr. with an Introduction by Frank G. Kirkpatrick, Atlantic Highlands, N.J.: Humanities Press, 1991; reissued, 1995).

Religion, Art and Science: A Study of the Reflective Activities in Man (Liverpool: Liverpool University Press, 1961).

Search for Reality in Religion (London: Allen and Unwin, 1965).

Further Reading

Costello, John E., *John Macmurray: A Biography* (Edinburgh: Floris Books, 2002).

Duncan, A.R.C., *On the Nature of Persons* (New York: Peter Lang, 1990).

Fergusson, D.A.S. and Dower, N., eds., *John Macmurray: Critical Perspectives* (New York: Peter Lang, 2002)

Harrison, Stanley M., ed., *Philosophy and Theology*, Special Issue, 6:4 (1992).

Lam, Elizabeth, 'Does Macmurray Understand Marx?', *Journal of Religion*, 20 (1940), pp. 47-65.

McIntosh, Esther, 'Reason versus Emotion: Redressing the Balance', *Practical Philosophy*, 4:2 (July 2001), pp. 28-32.

O'Connor, D.D., 'John Macmurray: Primacy of the Personal', *International Philosophical Quarterly*, 4 (1964), 464-484.

White, L.J., 'John Macmurray: Theology as Philosophy', *Scottish Journal of Theology*, 26 (1973), 449-465.